Reality 101

Authors:
Wayne Rice
David R. Veerman

Illustrator:
Chris Kielesinski

Contributors:
Rick Osborne
Ed Strauss
Karen Watson

Tyndale House Publishers, Inc.
Wheaton, Illinois

Library of Congress Cataloging-in-Publication Data

Rice, Wayne
   Reality 101 / Wayne Rice, David R. Veerman ; contributors: Rick Osborne, Ed Strauss, Karen Watson ; illustrator: Chris Kielesinski.
     p.   cm.
   ISBN 0-8423-3575-7 (sc : alk. paper)
   1. Teenager—Religious life—Miscellanea. 2. Christian life—Miscellanea. I. Veerman, David. II. Osborne, Rick.
III. Strauss, Ed. IV. Watson, Karen. V. Title. VI. Title: Reality one hundred one. VII. Title: Reality one hundred and one.
BV4531.2.R447 1999
248.8'3—dc21   98-43532

Printed in the United States of America

05 04 03 02 01 00
7   6   5   4   3

REALITY 101

CONTENTS

Acknowledgments x
Introduction xi

God Stuff

1. Why should we listen to what the Bible says? Wasn't it just written by people? 2
2. How can a book that was written thousands of years ago have anything to do with me? 4
3. Hasn't science proven that the Bible is wrong about a lot of stuff? 6
4. How did the Bible actually get written? 8
5. Why is the Bible so confusing to read? 10
6. Who decided what books went into the Bible? 12
7. How come during Bible times God did all these miraculous things like the burning bush and he doesn't do that today? 14
8. Why is the Bible so full of rules? Doesn't God want me to have any fun? 16
9. How is God three people and yet one God at the same time? 18
10. What makes one religion right and the others wrong? Aren't all religions just going to the same destination but following different roads to get there? 20
11. People talk about having a "relationship with God," but how can they have a relationship with someone they can't see? 22
12. Don't good people make it into heaven? 24
13. What about people who never hear about Jesus Christ? Will they go to heaven or hell? 26

Relative Issues

14. I'm old enough to make decisions and take responsibility for my life. Why won't my parents treat me like an adult and trust me? 30
15. My parents are so old-fashioned that they are an embarrassment to me. How can I get them to change? 32
16. The Bible says, "Honor your father and mother," but what if your parents aren't believers? 34
17. How do I introduce my parents to Christ? 36

18. Why do parents split up? 38
19. Why should my parents expect me to live like a Christian when I know they didn't at my age? 40
20. My stepparent is always telling me what to do. Why should I obey somebody who is not my real parent? 42
21. Why do brothers and sisters fight? 44
22. My parents keep asking me personal questions, but I don't want to tell them everything. Isn't it OK to have some privacy? 46
23. Our family vacations are boring. My parents say it's "family time." Why is that such a big deal? 48

Just Friends

24. I have trouble making friends. Is there something wrong with me? 52
25. How can I choose the right friends? 54
26. I have good friends, but my parents don't like them. What can I do? 56
27. My best friend is changing and starting to do things that I know are wrong and will hurt her. How can I help her stay on the right track? 58
28. Are all cliques bad? Is it wrong for my Christian friends to have a clique? 60
29. My closest friends like to go out and party. I don't! How do I keep their friendship without falling into their ways? 62
30. My friends don't go to church. Does that mean they will go to hell? 64
31. Is it safe to have non-Christian friends? Is it wrong? 66
32. Some of my friends put me down because I'm a Christian. What should I do? 68
33. How can friends who are Christians treat you so crummy sometimes? 70
34. My friends have spread rumors about me that aren't true. What should I do? 72
35. One of my friends has talked about suicide. Should I tell someone? 74

On the Horizon

36. How can I know God's will? 78
37. I have no idea what I'm going to do with my life. Nothing seems to interest me. What should I do? 80

38. Will God's plan always be something that I don't like? 82

39. What does it mean when people say, "Jesus is coming back"? How will he come back? 84

40. How do I know if what I want to do is what God wants me to do? 86

41. Is it true that we are not supposed to know about our future? 88

42. How can I know I'll find my perfect mate? Is there only one right person to be married to? 90

43. If you know God has everything under control, is it still OK to be disappointed? 92

44. What if I go to college and have a particular major but don't use it? 94

45. When you die, what happens? Do you go straight to heaven? 96

46. When I look at how adults have messed up the world, I get pretty discouraged. Am I destined to become just like them? 98

47. Should Christians be involved in protecting the environment for future generations if Jesus is coming back soon anyway? 100

Get Real

48. Will God love me more if I do everything right instead of messing up all the time? 104

49. Most of the time I wish I were someone else. Why did God make me this way? 106

50. How can I figure out what I'm good at? 108

51. I seem to act differently with different groups of kids. How can I tell which me is the real me? 110

52. How do you define a "bad" person? 112

53. People tell me I'm a loser. Why shouldn't I believe them? 114

54. Is it acceptable to change your appearance with plastic surgery, tattoos, body piercing, etc? 116

55. If drugs make me feel so good, why shouldn't I take them? 118

Big Bucks

56. Why do I always seem to need more money? 122

57. Is it OK to have a part-time job during the school year? 124

58. Is money itself bad (evil)? 126

59. Is it wrong to desire to live in a big house, have a nice car, and have expensive things? 128

60. Why is the church always asking for money? 130

61. How much money should I give to the offering? 132

62. Should I start saving money now for when I'm old and can't work anymore? 134

63. Is gambling wrong? 136

64. What's the point of working so hard for a few lousy bucks when all the really successful people are making millions? 138

Pump It Up

65. How does music affect me? 142

66. What's the difference between regular rock and Christian rock music? 144

67. Listening to rock music makes me feel good. What's wrong with that? 146

68. I listen to Christian rock: should I try getting my friends to listen to it? 148

69. What's wrong with seeing R-rated movies and videos? I've heard it all and seen it all before. 150

70. Does God have a sense of humor? 152

71. Is God OK with science-fiction books and movies? 154

72. If you know that swearing is wrong, it is really bad to hear it in movies? 156

73. Can Christians become entertainers in the secular world, or should they make only Christian music and Christian movies? 158

Getting Through

74. Since God knows everything, why should I pray? 162

75. How do I know if God hears what I pray? 164

76. Does God hear me if I pray in my head and not out loud? 166

77. How does prayer work? What difference does it make in the world? 168

78. Does God always answer our prayers? 170

79. What should we pray for/about? 172

80. Is there a right way and a wrong way to pray? 174

81. How come sometimes when I pray it feels like no one is there listening to me? 176

82. How long should I pray? Is praying once for one thing long enough? 178

83. People say, "God spoke to me in prayer." Should I hear God's voice talking to me? 180

The Class Act

84. Why do adults make such a big deal about grades? 184
85. Why do parents get so upset at one bad test if you still have a good grade in the class? 186
86. Will God be mad if I drop out of school? 188
87. Does God really help me when I pray before a test? 190
88. Is it illegal to take a Bible to class? 192
89. Should I disagree with my teacher when he teaches evolution? 194
90. How important is it to make your Christianity known in your school? 196
91. Why do I have to take all these stupid classes that I'll never use in the future? 198
92. My parents want me to go to college and only care about academics. Do I listen to my parents or do what I know is best for me? 200

Bad News

93. If God is love, why is there so much hate? 204
94. Why does God allow so much pain and suffering? 206
95. Since God can do anything, why doesn't he make things fair? I don't want special treatment; I just want things fair. 208
96. Why isn't the world any different since Jesus came and died? I thought that was supposed to change things. 210
97. Why did my parents' generation leave the world in such a mess? 212
98. What can one person my age do to make a difference in the world? 214
99. Will we be held responsible for things we didn't do as well as for things we did do? 216
100. Should Christians ever "pull the plug"? 218
101. What about capital punishment? 220

Special thanks to these youth directors and their students for helping us discover the questions to answer:

Nate Conrad
   Naperville Presbyterian Church—Naperville, Illinois

Kirk Dana
   Trinity United Methodist Church—Palm Beach Gardens, Florida

Cliff Heagy
   Zion United Church of Christ—Sheboygan, Wisconsin

Mary Ann Lackland
   North Phoenix Baptist Church—Phoenix, Arizona

Scott Peterson
   Berean Baptist Church—Burnsville, Minnesota

Kendra Smiley
   East Lynn United Methodist Church—East Lynn, Illinois

Mike Zegarski
   Young Life Naperville—Naperville, Illinois

HEY, when you get to be your age, you have questions—good questions—and you want answers.

Some adults get nervous when teenagers start asking questions. Maybe they see questioning as a lack of faith, especially if the questions are about God and his work in the world.

But questions are good. The Bible has tons of questions, some of them pretty tough. And God is never threatened by questions or upset with those doing the asking if they are sincerely looking for answers. Questions lead to answers, and answers lead to understanding and a deeper faith.

So here are 101 questions, asked by students just like you. We have also included answers and the source of those answers, God's Word.

Keep asking those questions . . . and keep looking for answers. How else are you going to learn?

Wayne Rice and
Dave Veerman

Q: Why should we listen to what the Bible says? Wasn't it just written by people?

A: Yes, the Bible was written by people—some very special people who were chosen by God to write what he wanted them to write. In other words, they didn't write it alone. Second Peter 1:21 says that the Holy Spirit "moved the prophets" (people who wrote the Bible) "to speak from God." They wrote with the inspiration of the Holy Spirit, under his guidance. God wanted to tell us about himself, his plan for us and our life, and about how we can get to know him. He wanted us to have a hard copy of his thoughts and ideas, so to speak, so he directed certain prophets and apostles to write them down. Human beings were the writers, but God was the author.

Bottom line: We listen to what the Bible says because it

is God's Word. If you believe in God, then it shouldn't be too difficult for you to believe that *(a)* God has communicated with us and *(b)* what he has to say is very important. But even if you don't believe, consider this: The Bible has stood the test of time. No other document has been around longer, influenced more people, or proven to be more reliable. Other writings come and go, but the Word of God will last forever (Matthew 24:35).

✔ reality check   Words that were "just written by people" can sound pretty ridiculous after a period of time. Consider these words that failed the test of time:

Every thing that can be invented has been invented.
—*Charles H. Duell, commissioner, U.S. Office of Patents, 1899*

The bomb will never go off. I speak as an expert in explosives.
—*Admiral William Leahy, U.S. Atomic Bomb Project*

I think there is a world market for maybe five computers.
—*Thomas Watson, chairman of IBM, 1943*

We don't like their sound, and guitar music is on the way out.
—*Decca Recording Company in a letter rejecting the Beatles, 1962*

A cookie store is a bad idea. Besides, the market research reports say America likes crispy cookies, not soft and chewy cookies like you make.
—*Response to Debbi Fields's idea of starting Mrs. Fields Cookies*

Remember, only God has the last word!

Word
from the
Word

Above all, you must understand that no prophecy in Scripture ever came from the prophets themselves or because they wanted to prophesy. It was the Holy Spirit who moved the prophets to speak from God. (2 Peter 1:20-21)

DIGGING DEEPER: *Jeremiah 1:9; 1 Thessalonians 2:13; 2 Timothy 3:16*

Q: How can a book that was written thousands of years ago have anything to do with me?

A: That's what makes the Bible unique. The Bible is God's Word; it is alive—because God is alive. Hebrews 4:12 says, "For the word of God is full of living power. It is sharper than the sharpest knife, cutting deep into our innermost thoughts and desires. It exposes us for what we really are." Far from being a dead book, the Bible has something fresh and relevant to say every time you open it. In other words, when you read the Bible today, it will speak directly to what you are experiencing today. If you read the same passage again a year from now, the same thing will happen. This occurs because the Holy Spirit helps us to interpret the Bible correctly and to apply it to our lives (John 14:17, 26; 15:26; 16:13). Remember, God is the author, and he never changes—the Bible contains God's timeless truths.

✔ reality check
Daniel was a young man who had been forced to move to another city. He had no reason to believe this move would be a positive experience. But before long, Daniel started to get noticed. Many people commented on his good looks. There was plenty of attention from young women. He began to be invited to parties that served fancy food and drinks. Finally he was invited to participate in an exclusive group at school. This group offered chances to move up in the world, but Daniel had not counted on some of the decisions he'd have to make.

Even though he'd always done pretty well in school, the demands of the new school would leave little time for worshiping God. The new crowd expected Daniel to go along with things he knew were wrong. He had a feeling that taking a stand could cost him everything. But how could he pass up this chance for a real future?

Sound like your life? Maybe the Bible could speak to you after all. This is the 2,500-year-old story of Daniel. Read Daniel 1 to see how he solved his problem.

Word from the Word

All Scripture is inspired by God and is useful to teach us what is true and to make us realize what is wrong in our lives. It straightens us out and teaches us to do what is right. (2 Timothy 3:16)

DIGGING DEEPER: *Psalm 119:9, 89-91; Matthew 4:4; 24:35; 1 Peter 1:24-25*

Q: **Hasn't science proven that the Bible is wrong about a lot of stuff?**

A: Actually, science has proven that the Bible is right more often than most people think. Archaeologists have located many of the sites mentioned in the Old Testament that skeptics previously thought to have been nonexistent. For example, in 1993 archaeologists uncovered a ninth-century B.C. inscription at an ancient mound called Tell Dan in northern Israel. Words carved into a chunk of basalt (type of rock) refer to the "House of David" and the "King of Israel."

Also, recent discoveries in physics have made it possible to understand biblical concepts that were previously very puzzling—such as how a day (from God's point of view) could be the same as a thousand years (see 2 Peter 3:8).

We need to keep in mind, however, that the Bible was written not to explain science and history but to reveal the nature and character of God. When we read about the six days of creation in the first chapter of Genesis, for example, the focus is not on how it was done but on who did it.

We should point out that science has not proven the Bible wrong with regard to creation. Scientists have only theories—educated guesses—about the origins of human beings and the universe. Amazingly enough, it often requires more faith to believe those theories than to believe the biblical version of creation.

It also helps to remember that some Bible stories describe miracles that God used at various times to demonstrate his power over nature. By definition, miracles are not very scientific, but then God, by definition, is greater than science. He created the natural world and has power over it.

✔ **reality check**
Sometimes science can help us understand important spiritual truth. One of the best examples is found in Psalm 103:12: "He has removed our rebellious acts as far away from us as the east is from the west." What would happen to this statement if you put north and south in place of east and west in this verse? North and south meet at the equator. East and west never meet because there is no east or west pole. God used scientific truth to help us get our brain around how far his forgiveness goes. Cool, huh?

Word
from the
Word

Though everyone else in the world is a liar, God is true. As the Scriptures say, "He will be proved right in what he says, and he will win his case in court." (Romans 3:4)

DIGGING DEEPER: *1 Corinthians 1:19-20; 1 Timothy 6:20*

Q: How did the Bible actually get written?

A: On an ancient Apple computer. (Just kidding!) Actually, the Bible was written over a period of about fifteen hundred years (from the time of Moses to shortly after the death and resurrection of Jesus) by more than thirty different writers. The true author was God. He inspired both the Old and New Testament writers to write all sixty-six books of the Bible that we have today (see 2 Timothy 3:16). The remarkable thing is that even though these writers did not collaborate with each other, the book they produced is unified and is the most important book in the history of humankind.

When we say that God "inspired" the writers of the Bible, we do not mean that God dictated every word as if the writers were secretaries. Instead, God allowed the writers to express their God-given thoughts in their own language, according to their own cultural situations and literary styles. The Old Testament was most likely first written on scrolls made of animal skins that were then copied over and over again by scribes, who had to do them by hand one at a time. There were no copy machines or printing presses in those days. The New Testament books were originally written on papyrus (an early form of paper) and again copied by scribes and preserved by Christians over the centuries. The Old Testament was written in the Hebrew language, and the New Testament in Greek.

Over the centuries archaeologists and others have found many parts of ancient copies of the Bible. When compared, these pieces of Scripture demonstrate the accuracy of the copying and the preservation process. God not only inspired the original writing, but he also made sure that the Scriptures were preserved throughout the centuries so that we would have them today.

✔ reality check
Have you ever played the game where a short story is whispered from person to person around the circle? It is amazing how quickly the story grows and the details change. This happens among people of similar age and experience over a *very* short period of time. The Bible was written by over thirty different writers over a period of fifteen hundred years. That's why the unity of the Bible is a strong piece of evidence that it is inspired by God. What a difference it makes when God whispers in your ear!

Word
from the
Word

So Jeremiah sent for Baruch son of Neriah, and as Jeremiah dictated, Baruch wrote down all the prophecies that the Lord had given him. (Jeremiah 36:4)

DIGGING DEEPER: *Exodus 31:18; Jeremiah 36:1-4, 17-18; 2 Peter 1:20-21*

Q: Why is the Bible so confusing to read?

A: The Bible may seem confusing at times because it was originally written in a different language from those we speak today. Many of the expressions people used during Bible times meant something completely different from what they do now. Also, for a long time the most widely read translations of the Bible were written hundreds of years ago in old English. Obviously, the precise meanings of many of those words have changed quite a bit over the years. That's why it's a good idea to read a modern translation of the Bible—it will be much easier to understand than the King James Version.

Another reason the Bible may seem confusing is that it is

a collection of individual books with different themes or purposes. It's like a library of books. For example, the Old Testament includes books containing history and law, then poetry and wisdom, and then prophecy. And these books don't always appear in chronological order. That's why it's a good idea to use Bible study tools (such as a study Bible and a good Bible commentary) to help you understand why each book was written and what the situation was at the time of its writing.

Perhaps the best way to make the Bible less confusing is to read it often. The more familiar you become with it, the easier it will be to understand. And, of course, if you know the Author personally, you will soon discover that the Bible isn't nearly as confusing as you thought.

✔ reality check

It is important to remember that even the disciples were sometimes confused. Jesus was teaching them things that were so radically different from the world they knew that sometimes they just didn't get it right away. The same is true for us today.

Jesus says, "Deny yourself." The world says, "Just do it." Jesus says, "The last will be first." The world says, "No one remembers second place." Jesus says, "Why worry about your clothes?" The world says, "Image is everything." Jesus says, "Love your enemies." The world says, "Get even."

The biggest problem isn't understanding what the Bible says. The challenge is living out what we learn from it.

Word
from the
Word

They read from the Book of the Law of God and clearly explained the meaning of what was being read, helping the people understand each passage. (Nehemiah 8:8)

DIGGING DEEPER: *Psalm 119:18, 27, 144; 2 Corinthians 4:4*

Q: **Who decided what books went into the Bible?**

A: Unlike most books, the Bible was not put together by one person or even by a small group of people. Over many years the Jews preserved and compiled the Old Testament Scriptures into what eventually became known as the Torah, the Jewish Bible.

Not long after the time of Jesus Christ, some of his disciples (apostles) wrote the four Gospels and the other documents that make up the New Testament. These documents were circulated among the churches and were read out loud during worship services. Eventually they became part of the Christian Bible. Other Christian writings were circulated at that time as well, but they were not considered to be the Word of God. By the end of the second century A.D., the twenty-seven books that are now in the New Testament had become accepted as Scripture, not because someone had declared them so, but because they were self-authenticating. In other words, God's people recognized God's voice in the books and recognized that over time the writings had proven themselves to be true. Later, in the fourth century, the leaders of the church made them official by declaring the canon (the set of Bible books) closed.

✔ **reality check**   Did you know that God's name is never mentioned in the Old Testament book of Esther? Some people think that the Song of Songs is too sexually explicit to be in the Bible. Even Martin Luther thought that the book of Revelation should not be included in the Bible since no one could understand it.

From a human perspective, reasonable arguments could be made for eliminating certain parts of Scripture, but imagine what we'd miss. The book of Esther shows how God can use the obedience of a few powerless people to save an entire nation. Song of Songs shows us Christ's devoted love for his followers. And though we may not understand the lampstands, dragons, and beasts in Revelation, God's promise to one day "remove all of [our] sorrows" (Revelation 21:4) is good news in a hurting world. In the same way that God guided the writers of Scripture, he also guided the process that put the books of the Bible together.

Word
from the
Word

Well then, why was the law given? It was given to show people how guilty they are. But this system of law was to last only until the coming of the child to whom God's promise was made. And there is this further difference. God gave his laws to angels to give to Moses, who was the mediator between God and the people. (Galatians 3:19)

DIGGING DEEPER: *Luke 1:1-4; Revelation 1:1-2; 19:9*

Q: **How come during Bible times God did all these miraculous things like the burning bush and he doesn't do that today?**

A: God used quite a few miracles in the Old Testament, primarily to communicate with his people and prove to them his power and love. You would think that with all the miracles God did everyone would have believed in him and served him, but they didn't. Even after a huge miracle like the parting of the Red Sea, the Israelites still rejected God and worshiped an idol—a golden calf (Exodus 32). God's people were no strangers to miracles back then, but they still turned their backs on him—numerous times—and were repeatedly unfaithful.

The greatest miracle of all was God's becoming a man—Jesus. When Jesus was on earth, he also used miracles to demonstrate the power and love of God. Most of his miracles were acts of kindness and compassion. Jesus healed people who were sick and even raised a few from the dead. Still, some of the people were not impressed. Many even demanded that Jesus be crucified.

Some people think that if God performed more public miracles today, everybody would believe in him and become a Christian. But history has proven otherwise. What God wants from us now is our faith in his power and love, even when we don't get miracles to prove them. Today we have God's Word, the Bible, and we also have the Holy Spirit, who lives in us and gives us power to live for Christ. Hey, wait a minute—that's a miracle right there!

✔ reality check

What would you be willing to trade from your life today to see a miracle? Would you give up your favorite shoes to get a pair that would last forty years? Would you be willing to never have another Big Mac in exchange for food you'd find on the grass in your front lawn each morning? The point is that most miracles aren't about razzle-dazzle. The miracles we see in Scripture happen when God intervenes in desperate situations to meet the needs of his people. Think about how God meets your needs from day to day!

Word
from the
Word

But despite all the miraculous signs he had done, most of the people did not believe in him. (John 12:37)

DIGGING DEEPER: *Exodus 3:1-4; Psalm 78:32, 40-43; Matthew 12:38-39; Luke 11:29-30; 16:27-31*

Q: Why is the Bible so full of rules? Doesn't God want me to have any fun?

A: Rules aren't bad. We need to live within limits. It's like the rules of a game. Why does baseball have so many rules? Don't they want the players to have any fun? How about all those rules in a basketball game or a football game?

Let's face it: If we took away all the rules, there wouldn't be a game at all, would there? Instead, chaos would reign, and nobody would have any fun. In games, when you break the rules you are penalized and sometimes put yourself in danger of losing the game. The boundaries and rules make the game make sense and fun to play. They're like instructions for a computer or an owner's manual for a car. The directions tell how the computer or car will run *best*.

When God created us, he gave us some rules to help us get the most out of life. God knows us perfectly, and he knows what we need in order to be and do our best. So God gives us rules and instructions for our benefit, to protect us and to give us "life in all its fullness" (John 10:10).

The Bible actually has surprisingly few rules. In the Old Testament you'll find the Ten Commandments, which form the foundation for ethical behavior in the entire civilized world. Nobody wants to live in a world where people cheat, steal, murder, and lie. In the New Testament Jesus summarized the law with just two rules—love God with all your heart, and love your neighbor as yourself (see Matthew 7:37, 39). Sure, the Bible has other rules for living, but they are there for our benefit, not to take away our fun.

✔ reality check

If you think some of *God's* rules are strange . . .

- In Nevada it's illegal to ride a camel on the highways.
- In Zion, Illinois, it's against the law to offer a cigar to a pet.
- In Minnesota it's illegal for a woman to dress up like Santa Claus on city streets.
- In Washington, D.C., bull throwing is strictly forbidden.
- In Wilbur, Washington, it's against the law to ride an ugly horse.
- In Idaho the law forbids one citizen to give another citizen a box of candy that weighs more than fifty pounds.
- Every citizen in Kentucky is required by law to take a bath once a year!

Word
from the
Word

Loving God means keeping his commandments, and really, that isn't difficult. (1 John 5:3)

DIGGING DEEPER: *Micah 6:8; Matthew 7:12; 22:36-40; Galatians 5:13-14*

Q: **How is God three people and yet one God at the same time?**

A: Christians believe in one God—God the Father, God the Son, and God the Holy Spirit. If you are confused by that statement, you are not alone. The doctrine of the Trinity has puzzled people for centuries. In fact, it is virtually impossible to understand. We accept the concept of the Trinity by faith because the Bible teaches it. Jesus said that he and the Father are "one" (John 10:30; see also 14:9-11). At Jesus' baptism, Jesus stood in the water, the Father spoke from heaven, and the Holy Spirit descended like a dove (Luke 3:21-22).

How can three be one? Some people have tried to explain it by using analogies. For example, water can take three forms—liquid, ice, and steam. All three are still water. That analogy is OK, but it falls apart because a specific body of water can't be liquid, ice, and steam all at the same time. God, on the other hand, is all three persons at once. Another common analogy involves the egg. An egg is made up of three parts: the shell, the white, and the yolk—three in one. Not bad, but it implies that God has parts, and it still doesn't convey that God is all three persons at the same time. He is not *part* Father, *part* Son, and *part* Holy Spirit. All three are God, not part of God.

Or try this one—you. Chances are, you play more than one role in life. You may be a student, a son or daughter, and an employee—all at the same time. In a sense, God is like that. The Father, Son, and Holy Spirit perform three different roles, yet they are still one God.

None of these analogies work perfectly, but they help point us to the truth, which is itself a great mystery.

✔ reality check Just be glad we didn't ask some
of these folks to try to explain the Trinity!

Hawaii is a unique state. It is a small state. It is a state that is by itself. It is a—it is different from the other forty-nine states. Well, all states are different, but it's got a particularly unique situation.
—*Dan Quayle, former U.S. vice president*

Be sure and put some of those neutrons on it.
—*Mike Smith, baseball pitcher, ordering a salad at a restaurant*

The word *genius* isn't applicable in football. A genius is a guy like Norman Einstein.
—*Joe Theismann, NFL quarterback and sports analyst*

A day without sunshine is like, you know, night.
—*Anonymous*

Word *from the* **Word**

The Father and I are one. (John 10:30)

But if I do his work, believe in what I have done, even if you don't believe me. Then you will realize that the Father is in me, and I am in the Father. (John 10:38)

DIGGING DEEPER: *Matthew 28:19; Luke 3:21-22; John 1:1, 14; 14:9-11*

Q: What makes one religion right and the others wrong? Aren't all religions just going to the same destination but following different roads to get there?

A: If you believe that, then you may as well start your own religion, one that you like, and make yourself the leader of it. In fact, many people have done exactly that. There are thousands of different religions in the world, many of them cults, and New Age religions have sprung up just in the last few years. Religions to suit your tastes are everywhere—even some that worship Satan.

But this is not new. Ever since God first created human beings, they have in turn created false gods and false religions. That's how people try to make themselves superior to God. But there is only one God and only one way to know him; all other religions lead not to eternal life with God but to death and eternal separation from God. Jesus didn't come to start a religion but to die for people so they could have their sins forgiven and live forever with him.

We know this because that's what God's Word, the Bible, says. How can you tell if a religion is right or wrong? Check it out against God's Word. The Bible is the only way to determine what is true and what is false. Without the Word of God, everyone is free to make up his or her own religion.

Even if people *sincerely* believe in another way to God, they are sincerely wrong. Jesus said that he was the *only* way: "I am the way, the truth, and the life. No one can come to the Father except through me" (John 14:6). Jesus doesn't sound very willing to leave room for other "ways," and neither should we as his followers. That's why we have missionaries and evangelists. Jesus commanded us to take the gospel to the whole world because without Christ, the world is lost.

Thank God there's one way.

✔ **reality check** Think about this group that followed a "different road" to get to God.

Between March 21 and 23, 1997, thirty-nine members of a group known as Heaven's Gate took their lives. They believed that committing suicide at the right time would release them from their "containers" and free them to be "replanted" in the containers of superior beings. They believed these new containers were aboard a UFO that was hidden behind the Hale-Bopp comet. Surviving members of the group continue to promote their faith through Web sites and mailings of audiotapes and videotapes.

Word *from the* **Word**

Jesus told him, "I am the way, the truth, and the life. No one can come to the Father except through me." (John 14:6)

DIGGING DEEPER: *Isaiah 43:10-11; 45:21-22; John 10:1-11; 1 Timothy 2:5*

Q: **People talk about having a "relationship with God," but how can they have a relationship with someone they can't see?**

A: Relationships involve communication, love, guidance, etc. God is a person and is described as "Father." We can talk with God through prayer; he talks to us through his Word, and he works *in* us.

Actually, we often have relationships with people we can't see. If you are separated from a loved one, it is still possible to have a relationship with that person—using letters, the phone, E-mail, or other forms of communication. In the same way, we can have a relationship with God using the ways we communicate with him and he with us—prayer, worship, the Bible, the preaching of his Word, etc.

It is true that we cannot see God, but "the heavens tell of the glory of God. The skies display his marvelous craftsmanship," says Psalm 19:1. That means that we can see evidence of God in his creation. In fact, we have evidence of God all around us.

We can see God in other people, in those who are part of his family. And, of course, we can see God in the person of Jesus Christ. God became visible when he became a man and "lived here on earth among us" (John 1:14). If you have trouble picturing what God is like, take a look at Jesus as he is revealed to us in the Bible. Jesus said, "Anyone who has seen me has seen the Father!" (John 14:9).

Remember, faith often means believing in something that we are unable to see (Hebrews 11:1). Jesus said to Thomas, "You believe because you have seen me. Blessed are those who haven't seen me and believe anyway" (John 20:29). God is not hiding from us, but he is a spirit and doesn't have a physical body that is limited to being in one place at one time.

It's easy to believe in something we can see. That requires no faith (and, hence, no effort) at all. But believing in God is an act of faith. And when we put our faith and trust in him, we enter a relationship with him that is as real as any other. Think of seeing God with your heart, not with your eyes. As we get to know God more and more and spend time with him, sincerely seeking his will and wanting to know him, he makes himself more and more real to us.

✔ **reality check** An older gentleman watched a small boy draw a picture. "What are you drawing?" he asked the boy.

"A picture of God," the little boy replied.

"But no one knows what God looks like," the gentleman said.

Without hesitation, the boy shot back, "They will when I get through!"

Word
from the
Word

You love him even though you have never seen him. Though you do not see him, you trust him; and even now you are happy with a glorious, inexpressible joy. (1 Peter 1:8)

DIGGING DEEPER: *Romans 1:20; Galatians 4:6; 1 John 3:1-2*

Q: Don't good people make it into heaven?

A: The real question here is, Just how good do you have to be to make it into heaven? We all know good people, but no one is totally good—perfect. So how good is "good enough"? That's a question the Pharisees asked Jesus over and over. His reply: "You are to be perfect, even as your Father in heaven is perfect" (Matthew 5:48). That's being *really* good. So the answer is yes—good people can make it into heaven *if* those good people can live without sinning even one time in their whole lives. The problem, of course, is that no one has ever done that . . . except for Jesus Christ. All human beings are born sinners; then they confirm that fact by sinning all the time. So no one is good enough except, of course, Jesus.

That has always been the problem with religions that stress "good works" or obeying religious rules and regulations. No matter how hard we try, we can't possibly be good enough. Nobody's perfect. Even the best person we know has a few flaws.

That's what makes Christianity unique. No religion except Christianity offers a solution to the problem of sin. Jesus came precisely for that purpose. He came to die for our sins, to make us good enough—perfect, in fact, so we can spend eternity with him in heaven.

✔ reality check

Should just "making it" to heaven be the goal? Some people say they aren't interested in going to heaven because they're not really sure they'd like it! Did you know that the Bible indicates that heaven won't be the same for everyone? The Bible tells of different rewards for believers and that some will just make it by the skin of their teeth (see 1 Corinthians 3:13-15).

In his book *The Great Divorce*, C. S. Lewis tells of a group of people on a bus ride to heaven. The story shows that if people aren't interested in spending time with and enjoying God while they are on earth, they probably won't enjoy heaven that much either. Read this short book; it will give you more "food for thought" on this issue.

Word *from the* **Word**

There is not a single person in all the earth who is always good and never sins. (Ecclesiastes 7:20)

DIGGING DEEPER: *Isaiah 64:6; Matthew 18:3; Romans 3:10, 23; 7:18*

Q: **What about people who never hear about Jesus Christ? Will they go to heaven or hell?**

A: Some people say that if a person doesn't hear about Jesus, he can't be lost because he's never had an opportunity to know him. If that were true, it would be better to never tell anyone about Jesus. Then no one could reject him. But that is not what God says. Scripture tells us to tell the news about Jesus to "every creature." Since we are told to tell everyone, we can assume that those who have not heard are lost.

Does that seem unfair? The Bible tells us in Romans 1:18-21 that what we see in creation gives "light," or understanding, about God to every creature. As someone desires to know more about God and his plan, God is faithful to reveal more about himself to that person. If someone responds to what God has already shown her (or him) about himself, God will bring the truth to that person's heart. Only those who reject the truth will be sent away.

God has made a big investment to help us know about his plan. He is a loving Father who wants all of his children to come to him and have eternal life. That's why God sent Jesus in the first place—to make it possible for people to get to heaven. If people could have gotten to heaven without trusting in Jesus Christ, then God wouldn't have sent Jesus at all. Jesus died for the sins of the world "so that everyone who believes in him will not perish but have eternal life" (John 3:16). It's our job as Christians to do everything we can to spread God's word.

✔ **reality check** Mission organizations are dedicated to reaching as many people as possible with the news of Jesus Christ. Some mission organizations even sponsor young athletes who travel to other parts of the world and compete with local teams. These athletes hold sports clinics, play demonstration games, and set up crusades where they tell about faith in Christ. Many countries no longer allow Christian missionaries to live there and openly share Christ. But these same countries welcome help from scientists, doctors, computer specialists, teachers, financial experts, and businesspeople. Christians can take advantage of these opportunities to share Jesus in these countries. How could God use your gifts and interests to help others learn about Jesus?

Word *from the* **Word**

But how can they call on him to save them unless they believe in him? And how can they believe in him if they have never heard about him? And how can they hear about him unless someone tells them? (Romans 10:14)

DIGGING DEEPER: *Matthew 18:12-14; Romans 2:12-16; 15:20-21*

Relative
Issues

#14

Q: I'm old enough to make decisions and take responsibility for my life. Why won't my parents treat me like an adult and trust me?

A: First of all, you need to realize that your parents have a hard time thinking of you as an adult because when they look at you, they can't help but see their cute little baby boy or girl, who at one time needed their help for everything. Other adults don't think of you that way, but your parents do. It takes time for parents to learn how to start treating you like an adult rather than like a little child who spills things and falls down a lot. Be patient.

Second, remember that trust must be earned. The more you show your parents that you can make good decisions and be responsible, the sooner they will get the idea that you can be trusted. Nobody gets trust for free. It's not something that everyone is automatically entitled to at a certain age. *Trustworthy people are trusted.*

Even though you are like an adult in some ways, you are still very young and have very few life experiences. If you prove to be trustworthy in small areas, your parents will begin to trust you with greater responsibilities.

✔ reality check
Adults have learned that no one is exempt from making bad decisions. Think about the not-so-great decision that led to this ad in the paper:

FOR SALE: Parachute. Only used once, never opened, small stain.

Parents know that life is full of faulty rip cords. They want to keep you from making the kinds of choices that don't leave room for second chances.

Word
from the
Word

The master was full of praise. "Well done, my good and faithful servant. You have been faithful in handling this small amount, so now I will give you many more responsibilities. Let's celebrate together!" (Matthew 25:21)

DIGGING DEEPER: *Luke 16:10-12; Colossians 3:20; 1 Timothy 4:12*

Q: My parents are so old-fashioned that they are an embarrassment to me. How can I get them to change?

A: Funny, your parents said the same thing about *their* parents. Your parents grew up in a different kind of world, so they sometimes have a hard time understanding yours. That's why parents are always saying things like "When I was your age. . . ." They remember what it was like when they were kids, and they sometimes have a hard time understanding that things are different today. It's doubtful that you can change them, and really, it's doubtful that you would want to see your parents wearing the same hairstyles, liking the same music, and wearing the same clothes that you and your friends do. That would be even *more* embarrassing.

But if you think your parents are totally out of touch with your world, try this. Show an interest in *their* world. Instead of cutting them off when they talk to you or putting them down when they express their opinions or ideas, listen and try to understand where they are coming from. They may just get the message and do the same for you!

Here's another suggestion: Help your parents by inviting them into your world from time to time. Don't worry about being embarrassed by them. Chances are pretty good that your friends aren't as embarrassed by them as you are. They may even think your parents are pretty cool.

By the way, if your parents said the same thing about you, what would you say? Shouldn't people be themselves? God tells us to love and accept others, even those who are different and who might be a little embarrassing.

✔ reality check
Sometimes it's really funny to see how your parents react to "fond memories" from their teenage years. Here's a trivia quiz you can give them based on bad songs from the '70s. This might make all of you lighten up a little!

1. Sing the chorus of "Feelings" by Morris Albert. *("Feelings, whoa, oh, whoa, feelings . . .")*
2. What group performed "You Should Be Dancing?" *(Bee Gees)* Bonus questions: Did you ever own a white, three-piece leisure suit? If yes, what kind of shoes did you wear with it? What color shirt did John Travolta wear with his? *(black)*
3. What was unusual about the song "Hooked on a Feeling" by Blue Suede? *(Featured the tribal-sounding chant, "Ooga chocka, ooga chocka")*
4. Complete this song title: "Me and You and a _____." *(Dog Named Boo)*

Word *from the* **Word**

So why do you condemn another Christian? Why do you look down on another Christian? Remember, each of us will stand personally before the judgment seat of God. (Romans 14:10)

DIGGING DEEPER: *Matthew 7:1-3; 1 Corinthians 13:4-7; Philippians 2:4*

Q: The Bible says, "Honor your father and mother," but what if your parents aren't believers?

A: The Bible doesn't qualify the commandment to honor and obey your parents with "if your parents are Christians" or "if your parents are wonderful people who deserve to be honored" or any other *if*. Children are simply commanded to honor their parents, period (Ephesians 6:2).

What does it mean to honor your parents? To honor someone means to give that person respect and acknowledge his or her authority. Parents don't have to be Christians to be respected. In the same way, God asks us to respect the laws of our government even though the government may not be a "Christian" government (Romans 13:1-7). All authority comes from God—even when that authority doesn't realize it is doing God's work.

The Bible also tells children to obey their parents (Ephesians 6:1). This can really be tough sometimes. It's against human nature to submit and obey, but that's what God tells us to do. It's the right thing to do. Jesus can help us be obedient if we ask him.

✔ reality check
Moses' father-in-law, Jethro, was a priest of Midian. Moses could have easily discounted Jethro and his influence and opinions. After all, Moses had been chosen by God to rescue an entire nation! Should Moses give a second thought to this ignorant nomad and his advice? Here's the story:

Jethro came into the Israelite camp and saw that Moses was totally stressed out by his responsibilities to the people. Moses was on a short track to total burnout! Jethro's advice (in true fatherly fashion) was: "What do you think you're doing? You're not going to last at this rate. Here's how you can get some help. . . ." Moses could have said, "Why should I listen to you, old man? You don't know God as well as I do." But he didn't. Moses respected his father-in-law and listened to him. Read Exodus 18 to get the whole story.

Word *from the* **Word**

Honor your father and mother. Then you will live a long, full life in the land the Lord your God will give you. (Exodus 20:12)

DIGGING DEEPER: *Deuteronomy 5:16; Mark 7:10; Romans 13:1-7*

Q: How do I introduce my parents to Christ?

A: The best way to introduce your parents (or anyone else) to Christ is by living in such a way that they will see Christ in you. St. Francis of Assisi once said, "Preach the gospel at all times; use words if necessary." He meant that words only enhance the message of a person's life.

Of course, that doesn't mean you have to be perfect. But if you are growing in your faith and if your parents are able to observe the changes—even the small ones—in your life, they may become interested. That's when you can tell them about your relationship with Jesus.

You can also invite your parents to go to church with you if they don't already attend. Or you might consider inviting them to a Christian concert or to a special event that your church is sponsoring (like a family fun night or other social activity).

Don't worry if your parents don't respond right away. Sometimes people have stored up many years' worth of negative feelings about God, Christianity, or the church, and overcoming those feelings takes time. Keep praying for your parents and do your best to honor them and show them that Jesus has made a difference in your life.

The Bible tells us to be ready to give an answer, to share our faith gently and lovingly with others when they ask. Being ready means knowing the gospel message and being able to tell it in your own words. If you aren't sure what to say, talk with your youth leader or another mature Christian. He or she will be happy to help.

✔ reality check

Remember, your parents have seen you go through a lot of phases, fads, and interests. They bought those soccer cleats (or tap shoes, or free weights, or musical instruments) that aren't really getting much of a workout today. How do they know that this is not just a passing thing for you? You may be asking "WWJD?" today, but they're wondering if tomorrow you may be back to "WCWYT?" (Who cares what you think?).

The direct approach of "Repent! You're on your way to hell!" will probably not be effective either. In fact, your parents may become hostile to the whole idea and wonder if you've cracked. Very few people like to be told by someone that their whole life has been a waste and that they're doomed—particularly if the person telling them still wants to be driven to the mall!

Ask God to help you be a consistent, attractive picture of Christ to your parents. Jesus said that anyone coming to him should count the cost. Your parents are watching to see if what you've "bought" pays off.

Word
from the
Word

Your godly lives will speak to them better than any words. They will be won over by watching your pure, godly behavior. (1 Peter 3:1-2)

DIGGING DEEPER: *Matthew 5:14-16; Luke 8:39; Philippians 2:14-15*

Q: **Why do parents split up?**

A: God's plan is for a husband and wife to stay together and not get divorced. When a man and a woman get married, they promise to stay with each other for life. They know it won't always be easy, but they want to work out their problems and stay together.

But all people are sinful and have weaknesses. No one is perfect. That is why troubles arise in all relationships, even between two people who love each other very much.

God wants Christians to stay married and work things out. He knows that when they do, their lives will be better for it. When arguments and other conflicts and pressures come, some people don't know how to handle them, so the problems get worse. Eventually these problems can become so big that the husband or the wife or both just give up and decide to end their marriage.

But sometimes parents do split up. The reasons are many (certainly too many to list here), and they are never easy to understand. If your parents are divorced or are going through a divorce, they may not even be able to explain exactly why it happened. They didn't plan for it or desire it, but they probably felt there was nothing left to do.

Still, it's natural to want to blame something or someone for a divorce. If your parents are divorced and you can't understand why, the easiest thing to do is to blame yourself. This is not the answer. The best approach is to avoid blaming anyone and do everything you can to demonstrate the love of Christ in the middle of a tough situation. Try to love and honor both of your parents even though they find it impossible to love and honor each other.

✔ reality check

A happy marriage is the union of two good forgivers.
—*Robert Quillen*

So many couples destroy each other because they are afraid to give up their right to be right.
—*David Stoop in* Seeking God Together

Word
from the
Word

This explains why a man leaves his father and mother and is joined to his wife, and the two are united into one. (Genesis 2:24)

DIGGING DEEPER: *Psalm 34:18; Malachi 2:14-16; Colossians 3:12-13*

Q: Why should my parents expect me to live like a Christian when I know they didn't at my age?

A: If your parents expect you to live like a Christian even though they were unable to do so when they were your age, consider that a compliment. They, of all people, know how difficult it is for a young person to make good choices and to avoid making serious mistakes. If they didn't believe in you, they wouldn't bother. You can feel sorry for kids whose parents don't think their children can be any better than *they* were.

Your parents may regret that they blew the opportunity to live for Christ when they were young. If they could turn back the clock, more than likely they would. They now see the results and consequences of their bad decisions and realize that God's way of doing things is always much better. They expect you to live like a Christian because they love you and want the best for you.

Be careful not to compare or to look for excuses. You should live like a Christian no matter what anyone else does, even Mom and Dad. Your parents are trying to do what is right.

✔ reality check

In 1978 a young man in his sophomore year of high school failed to make the varsity basketball team. Just four years later, that same young man nailed the winning basket in the 1982 NCAA championship game. Today, he's known as the greatest basketball player to ever have played the game.

Imagine Michael Jordan's father saying to his son in 1978, "Look, Michael, I didn't make the high school team either. It's no big deal. Why don't you just go down and hang out on the corner and forget it." Not likely, right? Mr. Jordan expected the best from his son. But no matter how much he believed in his son, the ultimate determination to succeed had to come from Michael's own heart. Somewhere along the line, Michael decided to devote himself to becoming the best basketball player he could possibly be.

To live as a Christian, you will have to decide at some point to devote yourself to becoming all that Christ wants you to be. As much as they might wish to, your parents can't make that choice for you. In the end, all they can do is support and encourage you.

Do you think Michael Jordan will encourage his son to do his best in whatever he does? You bet!

Word
from the
Word

Listen to your father's instruction. Pay attention and grow wise. (Proverbs 4:1)

DIGGING DEEPER: *Proverbs 4:1-3; 23:22; 1 Corinthians 10:1-11; Philippians 3:7-8*

#20

Q: My stepparent is always telling me what to do. Why should I obey somebody who is not my real parent?

> MY MOM AND STEPDAD TOOK ME SHOPPING LAST NIGHT. I GOT A LOT OF STUFF I NEED FOR SCHOOL. THEN WE WENT FOR DINNER, TOO. BOY, I CAN'T WAIT TILL THEY PAY FOR MY COLLEGE SO I CAN GO OFF AND BE MY OWN PERSON.

A: First, you should obey because he or she has authority over you and the Bible says that you should (Colossians 3:20). The apostle Paul did not make a distinction between "real" parents and stepparents. If your family includes a stepparent, then you are under the authority of both parents, not just your birth parent. The same rule would apply for kids who are adopted or who live in foster homes. Unless your parents are forcing you to commit a sin, you are expected to submit to the authority God has given to them.

Keep in mind that there is always a benefit for you. If you choose to disobey simply because your stepparent isn't your "real" parent, your life will not be better but worse. On the other hand, the more respect you give your stepparent, the more respect you will get in return. If you can establish a good relationship with your stepparent, you may receive more freedom and trust.

Remember, Jesus obeyed *both* his parents, and Joseph was his stepparent (Luke 2:51).

✔ reality check OK, so your new family isn't exactly

"The Brady Bunch." It's disappointing that your new stepparent isn't as cool, funny, and understanding as stepparents on TV shows. But here's a news flash for you—those shows aren't real life! Here are some words of advice from real kids who've lived through the same situation:

- Don't play dirty!: "A stepparent situation forces you to be so stinking mature! It's tempting to play one of them against the other to get what you want."
- Try a little kindness: "At first I didn't get along with my stepdad. But one day the thought hit me: *He's not a Christian. You ought to be a good example to him, and instead you're being so snotty!* So I decided to change. I started talking to him more, listening to him, even having conversations with him. I've noticed a change . . . that is improving things for the whole family."
- Don't have unrealistic expectations: "I think you have to look at your relationship with a stepparent more as a friendship relationship. They can't really take the place of your other parent. The most important thing is to let them know you respect them. And don't treat them like they don't belong."

(Adapted from *You Call This a Family?* by Gregg Lewis, with Tim Stafford, p. 58)

Word
from the
Word

If there is a problem between us, it is not because of a lack of love on our part, but because you have withheld your love from us. I am talking now as I would to my own children. Open your hearts to us! (2 Corinthians 6:12-13)

DIGGING DEEPER: *Luke 2:48-51; Colossians 3:20-25; 1 Peter 2:13-17*

Q: **Why do brothers and sisters fight?**

A: Most fights between brothers and sisters are normal. When people live together, they sometimes get annoyed with each other. They may try to use the same thing or want to occupy the same space, or maybe they want to do things differently. This happens in every family—even in families where people love the Lord and each other very much.

Brothers and sisters have been fighting since Cain killed his brother, Abel. One of the most common causes of fighting has to do with familiarity. Siblings know each other so well that they know how to push each other's buttons. Chances are you know how to make your brother or sister really angry, and this gives you a sense of power and superiority. But your brother or sister can do the same to you, which results in an endless battle that makes everybody's life miserable.

Another reason family members fight is a lack of respect for each other. We see each other all the time, so we know each other's flaws and shortcomings. Thus, we don't treat each other with the same dignity and respect that we give friends or even total strangers. Obviously something's wrong with that picture.

Even though you occasionally fight with your brothers or sisters, down deep you probably love them and would give your life for them. If someone tried to hurt them, you'd probably be the first person to come to their rescue, wouldn't you? Most brothers and sisters become friends as adults even though they fought a lot when they were children. It's a real sign of maturity to stop fighting and to learn how to show love to family members while you are still at home, living under the same roof.

One of the reasons God puts us into families is to teach us to get along with people—sometimes very difficult people—and to live his way in relationships. If we can get along at home, we probably will be able to get along anywhere.

Every conflict is an opportunity to learn one of life's most valuable skills—how to get along with others. The next time you disagree with a brother or sister, try to state your differences without yelling or hitting. If you are upset, calm down and lower your voice. Tell the other person how you feel. Try to see things from the other person's point of view. Listen to each other without interrupting. Then, as you talk it out, you can suggest a solution to the problem. Maybe you can take turns. Maybe you can give up a little of what you wanted. Remember, you're both on the same team.

✔ **reality check** From the new parent's dictionary: *Ow*—The first word spoken by a kid with an older brother or sister.

Word *from the* **Word**

Never pay back evil for evil to anyone. Do things in such a way that everyone can see you are honorable. Do your part to live in peace with everyone, as much as possible. (Romans 12:17-18)

DIGGING DEEPER: *Proverbs 15:1, 18; 17:9, 13-14; Romans 12:10; Ephesians 4:32*

#22

Q: My parents keep asking me personal questions, but I don't want to tell them everything. Isn't it OK to have some privacy?

A: The next time your parents ask you a personal question, try to remember that they are asking because they care a great deal about you. You can start worrying when your parents *stop* asking you personal questions. How much you tell them, of course, is entirely up to you. There's nothing wrong with having some privacy, but your parents need the assurance that you are OK. They remember that when you were little they had to watch you like a hawk to keep you from eating rat poison or sticking your finger in a light socket. Their worry is a sure sign that they love you.

If you never tell your parents anything, they will probably suspect the worst. And if you lie to them, they will find it difficult to trust you. That's why it's a good idea to trust your parents with the truth. If you do, they may stop asking you so many questions.

Be careful in this whole area of privacy, however. Some young people think that they should be able to do whatever they want, whenever they want, with no outside interference. But God has given your parents authority over you for a reason. He wants to teach you many lessons to prepare you for adulthood. This includes being mentored by your parents and other Christian leaders and learning to submit to authority. So privacy should be an issue only as far as it relates to the healthy, honest, private thoughts and moments that we all have concerning ourselves and our feelings.

✔ **reality check** Maybe you feel as if you're always on the hot seat. Try turning the tables on your parents with these:

1. Tell me one thing you did wrong as a kid for which you never got caught. (Honesty counts for ten points.)
2. What do you do when I'm at school?
3. Tell me about when you met Mom (or Dad).
4. Who was the first person you ever kissed? Describe the scene. Who initiated the kiss?
5. Describe your two closest friends when you were my age.
6. Did you ever have a boss you didn't like?
7. What really bugs you?
8. What have you done that really makes you proud?
9. Which emotion is the hardest for you to express? Why?
10. If you knew you were going to die tomorrow, what would you want to say to me today?

(From *Alive 2* by S. Rickly Christian, p. 99)

Word
from the
Word

That is why, when I could bear it no longer, I sent Timothy to find out whether your faith was still strong. I was afraid that the Tempter had gotten the best of you and that all our work had been useless. (1 Thessalonians 3:5)

DIGGING DEEPER: *Psalm 139:1-7; Proverbs 13:24; 2 Corinthians 1:24; 1 Thessalonians 2:11-12*

Q: Our family vacations are boring. My parents say it's "family time." Why is that such a big deal?

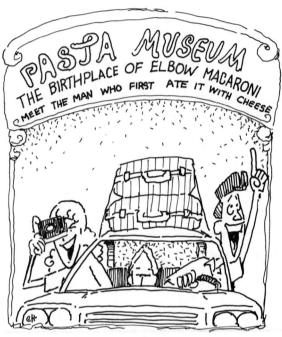

A: When you are older, you will probably remember those "boring" family vacations differently from the way you do now. Right now, you would probably rather be with your friends and have fun with them than go on a vacation with your family. But someday you'll be glad you had that "family time." Some families never take vacations together. Some parents are so busy with their work that they don't have time for a vacation. As a result they sometimes lose touch with their kids, and the family grows apart. God put us in a family, and it is our job to do whatever we can to keep the family close. A family vacation is one of the ways that we do that, even when it doesn't seem very exciting.

If your family does the "same old, same old" every year, you might suggest some new activities for your family to do. Your family may not be able to afford a trip to Hawaii or Disney World, but there are lots of other things to do, even close to home, that can be a lot of fun. Sometimes parents are open to allowing their kids to bring a friend along on a family vacation. You might suggest that idea. But whatever you do, make the most of it. Don't make a "boring" vacation even worse by complaining about it and making everybody else miserable. Even the most boring vacation can be fun if you have the right attitude.

Remember, you have only one family, and time passes quickly. Your parents love you and want to be with you. They know that soon you will be grown and gone. It's a big deal to them. Also remember that friends come and go but family is yours for life. Today many adults have no idea of the whereabouts of the friends they had in school, but they still see their brothers, sisters, and parents.

✔ **reality check** So you think your car trips are hot and crowded? On June 13, 1920, the U.S. Postal Service made it illegal to transport a person by the postal system.

Just imagine being slotted for a solo summer trip to Aunt Betty's in Death Valley!

Word
from the
Word

"Young and old, all of us will go," Moses replied. "We will take our sons and daughters and our flocks and herds. We must all join together in a festival to the Lord." (Exodus 10:9)

DIGGING DEEPER: *1 Samuel 20:6; Job 1:4-5, 18-20; Luke 2:41-45*

Q: I have trouble making friends. Is there something wrong with me?

A: Probably not. Everyone is different. Some people are introverts, and some are extroverts. Extroverts find it easy to make friends because they are so outgoing. Introverts have a more difficult time because they enjoy being alone or just having one or two close friends. There's nothing wrong with being an introvert if that's what you are. It's like being right-handed or left-handed. Right-handed people do things differently from left-handed people, and vice versa. That's not bad—just different.

On the other hand, there are some things you can do to make (and keep) friends. The most important thing is to be a friendly person. In other words, to *have* a good friend, you need to *be* a good friend. Don't act unfriendly by putting people down or being selfish or mean. Instead, do nice things for other people and treat them with respect. Everyone likes to be around people who are friendly and who make them feel good.

To find a friend, watch for someone who likes some of the same things you do and get to know that person. Don't expect him or her to come to you. If you want a friend, you will need to take the initiative to get to know someone. If that person doesn't become a close friend, don't worry. Sometimes it takes a while before you find the right person to be your friend.

If you experience rejection over and over, you might want to ask people who know you well (like your mom and dad, your youth pastor, or a teacher) if they have any ideas for you. Sometimes other people who can be honest with you can help you learn why you are having trouble making friends or if there is something you can do to improve your chances.

Remember, Jesus wants to be your friend too. He is a friend who "sticks closer than a brother" (Proverbs 18:24). With Christ as your friend you will be part of a family of others who also know him. That's a good place to develop friends. That's what the church (and your youth group) is all about.

✔ **reality check** Just wondering. . . . If Barbie is so popular, why do you have to buy her friends?

Word *from the* **Word**

When others are happy, be happy with them. If they are sad, share their sorrow. Live in harmony with each other. Don't try to act important, but enjoy the company of ordinary people. And don't think you know it all! Never pay back evil for evil to anyone. Do things in such a way that everyone can see you are honorable. (Romans 12:15-17)

DIGGING DEEPER: *Proverbs 17:17; 18:24; 20:6*

Q: How can I choose the right friends?

A: The first step in choosing good friends is to have a correct view of who *you* are. The way you think about yourself will determine the kinds of friends you choose. Your friends reflect your own self-image. In other words, if you think of yourself as a loser, you will probably choose losers for friends. If you think of yourself as a winner, however, you will choose winners for friends. So the first question to ask is, Who am I?

For example, if you are a Christian, you will want to find friends who are also Christians. If you think of yourself as a responsible, mature person, then you will want to have friends who also think of themselves that way. If you believe that certain behaviors (such as doing drugs and alcohol, participating in vandalism, or being sexually promiscuous) are wrong, then you will want to choose friends who share your values and beliefs.

Think of friendships in terms of assets and liabilities. An asset is positive; a liability is negative. When you choose a friend, ask yourself, Will this person be an asset or a liability to me? That is, will this person make a positive contribution to your life or just drag you down? Avoid friendships that will become liabilities in your personal and spiritual growth.

Finally, look for friends in the right places. Some places attract the wrong kinds of people. You don't want to find your friends there—it's too risky.

✔ reality check Three Ways to Tell You May Have
Chosen the Wrong Friend:

1. The juvenile judge has memorized your friend's address.
2. Your friend shops the mall in July wearing a trench coat.
3. Your friend considers a can of spray paint standard equipment for an evening of fun.

Word
from the
Word

Anyone who fears you is my friend—anyone who obeys your commandments. (Psalm 119:63)

DIGGING DEEPER: *Proverbs 12:20; Malachi 3:16*

#26

Q: I have good friends, but my parents don't like them. What can I do?

MOM!
DAD!
MEET MY
BEST
FRIENDS.

COSTUME
PARTY
SCHEDULE

CK.

A: Perhaps the first thing you should do is find out why your parents don't like your friends. Maybe your parents know something you don't.

If you have no idea why your parents don't like your friends, *ask*. You don't have to agree with your parents' opinions, but you really should listen and take their criticisms seriously. Do all you can to explain to your parents why you like your friends and why your friends are such good friends. Keep the communication lines open, and in time your parents may begin to see your point of view and change their mind. Help them get to know your friends. When you talk with your parents, listen. Don't argue; they may have special insights.

If your parents dislike your friends because your friends are not Christians, you might assure them that you plan to influence your friends more than they will influence you. Then follow through on that plan. Invite your friends to church or to youth group, and be very clear with your friends about your standards, values, and beliefs.

It's possible that your parents would change their opinion of your friends if they were to get to know them better. See if your parents would let you bring your friends along on a family activity, spend the night at your house on a weekend, or have dinner with the family. Sometimes parents make quick judgments about people (as we all do) when they don't know them.

If you have tried everything you can to help your parents understand your point of view and they still insist that you end a particular friendship, you have no choice, as a Christian, but to obey them. If you continue the friendship, you may be communicating to your parents that your friend is more important to you than they are. While you may feel that way right now, in the long run you will regret making that choice. It may be better to put the friendship on ice for a while (or keep it very low profile) and wait for a better time to discuss it with your parents again. Remember that friends are rarely forever, but your family is.

✔ **reality check** Parents can sometimes misjudge your friends. Did you hear the story about a guy named Jonathan? Jonathan's best friend was over for dinner and his dad tried to *kill* the friend. By the way, Jonathan's friend was the future king David. Jonathan's father, King Saul, tried to pin David to the wall with a spear!

Read 1 Samuel 18–20 to find out how Jonathan handled the situation.

Word *from the* **Word**

Young people who obey the law are wise; those who seek out worthless companions bring shame to their parents. (Proverbs 28:7)

DIGGING DEEPER: *Proverbs 10:1; 15:20; 23:22, 24; 29:3*

#27

Q: My best friend is changing and starting to do things that I know are wrong and will hurt her. How can I help her stay on the right track?

A: Your concern is a sign that you are a truly great friend. If your best friend hasn't gone too far, you need to encourage her to start making good decisions and to stay away from things that will only drag her down.

You can also set a good example for her by making good choices yourself. If you are really concerned about your friend and feel certain that you are strong enough to set a good example for her, you will want to stay close to her and be a good listener and encourager. Don't put your friend down by condemning her or making her feel shame for what she has done. In most cases that only makes people hurt themselves even more. Instead, offer your friend support and love and encourage her to walk away from the behaviors that are harmful to her. That's what friends are for. Friends can hold each other accountable during times of temptation or failure.

But if your friend is involved with something that is putting her life in danger, such as drugs or alcohol, then you have a respon-sibility to make sure she gets the help she needs. Encourage her to tell her parents, a school counselor, or your youth pastor or minister at church. If she refuses to do so, you may need to let her know that *you* are going to inform someone who can help her, not because you are a snitch, but because you are her friend and you care about her.

Be careful that your friend doesn't persuade you to join her in doing things that are wrong. If you are having trouble resisting the pressure to participate in those activities, it may be time to end your friendship. It's better to lose a friend than to lose your self-respect—and maybe even your life.

✔ **reality check** Hugh Herr and Jeff Batzer were world-class mountain climbers starting out on a weekend of ice climbing in New Hampshire. The first day of the climb they were trapped by a driving blizzard, lost and unable to find a trail in the waist-deep snow. After two days with no word from them, a massive search was begun. The continued bad weather made the searchers turn back. Fortunately these two young men had a friend in Melissa Bradshaw. She knew the area well and refused to give up. Five days after Hugh and Jeff disappeared, Melissa found tracks that led her to the huddled, half-frozen pair (*Reader's Digest*, Sept. 1983).

Sometimes we don't realize we're headed off the spiritual trail. Having someone like Melissa who cares enough to seek us out and help us find the way back can mean a lot.

Word
from the
Word

Dear brothers and sisters, if another Christian is overcome by some sin, you who are godly should gently and humbly help that person back onto the right path. And be careful not to fall into the same temptation yourself. (Galatians 6:1)

DIGGING DEEPER: *Psalm 119:61, 63; Proverbs 1:10; 27:6, 17; James 5:19-20*

#28

Q: Are all cliques bad? Is it wrong for my Christian friends to have a clique?

A: No, not all cliques are bad. A clique is basically a friendship cluster—a group of people who enjoy being together. There's nothing wrong with that. Circles of friends are OK.

Clique has become a negative term, however, because it usually describes a group of friends who shut other people out and sometimes use their power to bully other people or to destroy youth meetings, classes, and other activities. If that is what you mean by *clique,* then, yes, that kind of clique is bad, and it would be wrong for Christian friends to form such a group.

If you are part of a clique, you can make it a good Christian clique by keeping it open to new members and using your power and influence to help others and make your meetings and activities a success. Be a positive example of how a Christian should act by reaching out to others, not shutting them out.

✔ reality check   Beware! Keeping your friends from

becoming a negative, exclusive clique will take a lot of maturity on your part. Things will change when a new person comes into the group. Everything will suddenly feel different. The new person won't get all the inside jokes. She may hit it off with your best friend. Suddenly you hear they've gone to the mall without you. Or, guys, he may be a good athlete who is also trying out for a place on the team. What if he makes it and you don't? Are you starting to get the picture?

It can be easy to use cliques as a way of feeling comfortable and OK about yourself. But being a Christian isn't about shutting doors and keeping people at a distance. It's about giving someone a chance when you're not too sure they deserve it. That's what the Bible calls grace. Being alone is a pretty bad feeling, isn't it? In fact, it was the first thing on earth that God called "not good" (Genesis 2:18).

Word
from the
Word

When one of you says, "I am a follower of Paul," and another says, "I prefer Apollos," aren't you acting like those who are not Christians? (1 Corinthians 3:4)

DIGGING DEEPER: *Luke 9:49-50; Acts 20:29-30; 1 Corinthians 3:1*-6, 21-23

Q: My closest friends like to go out and party. I don't! How do I keep their friendship without falling into their ways?

A: If your friends are participating in illegal or harmful activities, you should do all you can to persuade them to stop. If they won't listen to you, then you may not be able to keep their friendship. You may need to seek out some new friends who share your values and beliefs.

If you still want to keep their friendships, keep this in mind: Real friends don't pressure each other to do what they don't want to do. If you don't want to party the way they do, then don't. Respectfully and politely explain that you don't want to go. If they don't accept that, they probably aren't very good friends. Friends worth keeping will respect your right to be yourself. If they try to force you to do something you don't want to do in order to be their friend, then drop 'em like a hot potato. They aren't friends worth keeping.

✔ reality check Don't try these seven really dumb ways to say no:

- "Sorry, I can't. It's my dog's birthday."
- "Wish I could, but it's my night to alphabetize our canned food."
- "Thanks for asking, but my mom can track like a bloodhound."
- "Can't. It's time for my favorite infomercial."
- "Did I tell you I'm thinking about trying out for a spot on the Extreme Fishing Team? Gotta tie some lures."
- "Guess I'll have to pass. If my room's not clean by the time my parents get home, they're calling City Sanitation."
- "My dad said we're having a man-to-man talk on the use of duct tape tonight."

Word
from the
Word

We should be decent and true in everything we do, so that everyone can approve of our behavior. Don't participate in wild parties and getting drunk, or in adultery and immoral living, or in fighting and jealousy. (Romans 13:13)

DIGGING DEEPER: *Proverbs 1:10; 2:12-15; 25:26; Romans 13:11-14*

#30

Q: My friends don't go to church. Does that mean they will go to hell?

> WE'VE BEEN SHIPWRECKED AND LOST FOR FOUR DAYS NOW. WE'RE OUT OF FOOD, WE HAVE NO WATER, AND HERE COME THE **SHARKS!**

> AND THE **WORST** PART IS, IF THEY DON'T FIND US BEFORE SUNDAY, WE'LL MISS CHURCH. THEN WE'LL **REALLY** BE IN TROUBLE.

A: Not necessarily. Church attendance isn't required to go to heaven. The church was God's idea, so church attendance is good and for our benefit. Christians should be part of a church community. But church attendance in itself won't keep you out of hell or get you into heaven. Heaven is only for those who put their faith in Jesus Christ, asking him to forgive their sins and trusting him to save them. When someone does that, that person becomes "born again," and you can't become "un-born again" by not going to church. Hopefully, though, people who truly believe in Christ and accept him as Savior will want to attend church so that they can grow, worship God, be with other Christians, and find ways to serve God.

There's still time for you to share Christ with your friends. If you or someone else can lead your friends to Christ, then they won't go to hell.

✔ **reality check** "Going to church doesn't make you a Christian any more than going to a garage makes you an automobile." (Billy Sunday)

Here is how kids your age answered a Gallup survey on heaven, hell, church attendance, and belief in Christ:

Do you believe there is a heaven? Yes—91% No—6%

Do you believe there is a hell? Yes—76% No—17%

What do you believe about Jesus Christ? He is God or the Son of God—86% Never lived or not sure—8%

How often do you read the Bible alone? Frequently or occasionally—44% Hardly ever or never—56%

How often do you pray alone? Frequently or occasionally—74% Hardly ever or never—25%

Have you ever personally experienced the presence of God? Yes—29% No—65%

Did you attend church or synagogue in the last seven days? Yes—48% No—52%

Now think about these questions: (1) Why do you think more people believe in heaven than in hell? (2) If most teens (65%) say they've never experienced the presence of God, why do they pray? (3) Do you think most people are open to the idea of a relationship with God? Why? (4) If most kids don't read the Bible, where do they get their ideas about Jesus and issues of faith?

Word *from the* **Word**

For if you confess with your mouth that Jesus is Lord and believe in your heart that God raised him from the dead, you will be saved. (Romans 10:9)

DIGGING DEEPER: *Acts 2:41-42, 46; 16:21-32; Hebrews 10:25*

#31

Q: **Is it safe to have non-Christian friends? Is it wrong?**

A: Yes, it's usually safe and, no, it's not wrong. Christians should have non-Christian friends so they can share their faith with them. In fact, Jesus was called "a friend of the worst sort of sinners" (Luke 7:34). Jesus hung out with some of the most despised people of his time. He did it for two reasons. First, he loved everybody. He didn't love religious people any more than he loved anyone else. We also should love people who are not Christians. You can have wonderful relationships with non-Christians because they, just like everyone else, are people made in the image of God.

Second, Jesus wanted to give those people eternal life and a relationship with him. We should want to do the same. As a Christian you are in a position to influence your non-Christian friends to become followers of Jesus Christ. That's why Jesus called his followers salt and light. The idea here is that we are to influence our friends in the world *more* than they influence us. There is potential danger, of course. If you feel that your friends are having a negative influence on you, then it may be time to find some new friends.

Remember, however, that our *closest* friends should be Christians (see 2 Corinthians 6:14-15). In other words, people you choose for heart-to-heart relationships—where you and your friends inspire one another; encourage one another; share your deepest feelings, thoughts, and aspirations; and spend a lot of time together—should be Christians.

✔ reality check "A guy named Dave saved my life."

That's how the testimony of Clym Escudero begins. Clym tells how Dave Tweeten, an ordinary eighth-grade guy, befriended him in school. Over the next three years of football practice, algebra class, choir, and regular day-to-day living, Clym began to ask Dave questions about becoming a Christian. Before long, Clym was a "brother in Christ."

Clym says, "I'm glad Dave didn't get on a soapbox and preach at me or reject me because I wasn't a Christian. Most of all I'm thankful he was willing to show me how a Christian is supposed to live."

Ask Dave how he "led" Clym to Christ, and he'll shrug and say, "I guess I was his friend. That's all. I was just his friend."

(From "Mission Possible: Sharing Faith with Your Friends" by Clym Escudero, with Chris Lutes, *Campus Life*, July/August 1996, p. 21)

Word
from the
Word

When I am with the Gentiles who do not have the Jewish law, I fit in with them as much as I can. In this way, I gain their confidence and bring them to Christ. But I do not discard the law of God; I obey the law of Christ. (1 Corinthians 9:21)

DIGGING DEEPER: *Mark 2:15-17; Luke 7:34-35; 1 Corinthians 5:9-11; 10:27*

#32

Q: **Some of my friends put me down because I'm a Christian. What should I do?**

A: If people put you down for being a Christian, be happy (Matthew 5:11-12). Thank God for the privilege (Acts 5:40-42), and keep loving and praying for those who put you down (Matthew 5:43-44). The Bible sometimes describes getting put down for your faith as persecution. It also says that you can expect to be persecuted (2 Timothy 3:12). Persecution is normal, and in a strange way, it's actually positive. It can indicate that you are being faithful to Christ. It's almost an identifying characteristic of Christians. When persecuted, the best thing to do is to pray for those who are persecuting you and to remain strong in your faith. Remember that when you respond well, demonstrating Christian behavior and love, your persecutors will see Christ in you and may be drawn to him (see Romans 12:17-21).

Some people say that they are being persecuted for being Christians when, in fact, people dislike and reject them because of their insensitive or foolish actions. If, for example, you were to stand on a table during lunch, pull out a Bible, preach, and declare that everyone in the room is a sinner bound for hell, you would probably be criticized, mocked, and even punished for your actions. The negative reaction from students, faculty, and staff would have little to do with your being a Christian. You would suffer not because of your faith but because you were being obnoxious and disruptive. That's an extreme example, but you get the point. Christians should demonstrate the highest character and be loving and kind to others. Some questions to ask are: Who or what is being persecuted here? Is it Christ and Christianity? Is it the way you are representing Christ? Is it your inability to reasonably present and defend your faith?

If your friends are putting you down for your faith in Christ, they aren't very good friends. But if you want to help those friends, you might try inviting them to a youth-group activity or a Christian concert or find some other way to show them what your faith is all about. They may even become Christians themselves.

✔ **reality check** Being put down feels pretty rotten, doesn't it? Sometimes in a group where you are the minority, it is easy to become the "punching bag." When that happens, it is usually because your friends don't want to risk admitting that they may be pretty insecure about themselves. In cases like that it is difficult to defend your faith effectively. Try to avoid getting caught in those situations. Never go along with the put-downs when someone else is the "punching bag." Make sure that you get involved in groups where your faith is accepted and encouraged. Continue to be who you are. Look for chances to share your faith with your friends in one-on-one situations.

Word *from the* **Word**

There are "friends" who destroy each other, but a real friend sticks closer than a brother. (Proverbs 18:24)

DIGGING DEEPER: *Luke 6:22-23; 1 Peter 3:9-17*

Q: How can friends who are Christians treat you so crummy sometimes?

A: No one is perfect, including Christians. So Christian friends can have off days or be insensitive and treat you crummy.

When you become a Christian, you don't automatically stop doing things that hurt other people. Christians are nothing more than crummy people (sinners) who have found new life in Christ. As we grow stronger in our faith, we gradually become a little less crummy and learn how to be more like Christ. But it takes time. Meanwhile, we have to accept each other with all our faults and learn how to forgive each other. Sometimes people do hurtful things to each other without even realizing it. As Jesus prayed when he was hanging on the cross, "Father, forgive these people, because they don't know what they are doing" (Luke 23:34).

When a Christian friend treats you poorly, first pray for that person and for your relationship with him or her. Ask God to give you wisdom and insight into how to get along with others. Second, talk to that Christian friend and explain, gently and unaccusingly, how you feel, giving room to hear the other side of the story. Third, forgive and ask for forgiveness where necessary. Always learn from the experience, and move toward closer relationships with your friends.

✔ **reality check** Sometimes it's easier to *talk about* praying for people who've hurt us than to actually do it. Have you ever been tempted to pray like this?

> May those who love us, love us;
> And those who don't love us
> May God turn their hearts;
> And if He doesn't turn their hearts,
> May he turn their ankles,
> So we'll know them by their limping.

(From *Be a People Person* by John Maxwell, pp. 18–19)

This is a great example of how *not* to build relationships!

Word
from the
Word

Whenever we have the opportunity, we should do good to everyone, especially to our Christian brothers and sisters. (Galatians 6:10)

DIGGING DEEPER: *Psalm 55:12-14; Luke 23:34; 2 Timothy 1:15; 4:10*

Q: My friends have spread rumors about me that aren't true. What should I do?

NOT ONLY DID HE END UP WITH A DEPT OF OVER TEN THOUSAND DOLLARS, BUT HE WAS IN AND OUT OF JAIL EIGHT TIMES.

A: Your first action should be prayer. Ask God for strength to endure the false rumors and for wisdom and courage to respond in the right way.

Next, talk with those who are spreading the rumors. Let them know, one on one or in a small group, that you don't appreciate it. Ask them to stop and set the record straight. Speak calmly but firmly, letting them know how you really feel. If they are really your friends, they will listen respectfully and respond accordingly.

If the rumor is untrue regarding particular facts, you probably need to find out who started the rumor and make sure that person knows the truth. For example, if someone is spreading a false rumor that you are going to break up with your boyfriend or girlfriend, you need to find out who is spreading that rumor and get those people to stop. You may also need to do a little damage control by telling those who are affected by the rumor (your boyfriend or girlfriend in this case) that the rumor is not true. Eventually people will find out the truth.

Other kinds of rumors aren't so easy to deal with. For example, if people are saying unkind things about you because they want to ruin your reputation or hurt you, there may not be anything you can say or do to stop them. Usually people who are trying to hurt you will keep spreading the rumor even though they know it is not true. All you can do is confront them and request that they stop. What you should avoid doing is spreading untrue rumors about the rumor spreaders. That only makes things worse, not better. The best thing to do is to let people know that the rumor is not true and then ignore it. If the rumor is an attack on your character, you should conduct yourself in such a way that your behavior proves that the rumor is false.

✔ reality check   When rumors are getting you down, be thankful someone isn't "digging you up":

Abraham Lincoln's coffin was pried open twice. The first time was in 1887, twenty-two years after his assassination. Why? Because of a rumor sweeping the country that his coffin was empty. Witnesses observed that the rumor was totally false. By 1901 the same rumors were circulating again and had planted doubts in the public's mind. Though Lincoln's family protested, the same ghoulish ceremony was repeated. Finally, the controversy was laid to rest as the president was buried in a crypt in Springfield, Illinois.

(From *Growing Strong in the Seasons of Life* by Chuck Swindoll, p. 105)

Word *from the* **Word**

It is God's will that your good lives should silence those who make foolish accusations against you. (1 Peter 2:15)

DIGGING DEEPER: *Proverbs 11:13; 16:28; 1 Peter 2:12, 21-23; 3:9-17*

#35

Q: One of my friends has talked about suicide. Should I tell someone?

A: We should always take talk of suicide seriously, even when someone seems to be joking. Yes, you should tell someone about it—a person who can help (a school counselor, parent, youth leader, teacher, etc.). If you have reason to believe that your friend is seriously considering suicide, you need to tell someone quickly.

How do you know if the person is serious? Here are a few clues:

1. If your friend has just experienced a very difficult personal crisis, like parents divorcing or a breakup with a boyfriend or girlfriend.
2. If your friend is hurting himself or herself in any other way, such as drug abuse, self-mutilation, or other high-risk behaviors.

3. If your friend seems unusually "low" (depressed) or unusually "high" (excited). Extreme mood swings often indicate that something is wrong.
4. If your friend wants to give you some of his or her prized belongings.
5. If your friend talks about a specific method of committing suicide or has access to a specific method (like a gun or sleeping pills)—definite danger.
6. If your friend has written a suicide note—extreme danger.

Sometimes you just have to go with your gut feelings when someone talks about suicide. On occasion, people will talk about suicide simply as a way of expressing their hurt, anger, or pain. Encourage your friend to get help, and offer to go with him or her to get it. But don't think you have to handle it by yourself. Call your pastor, youth pastor, or even the police. Your friend's parents should also know about this. If you know of a suicide hot line in your community, call it, and they will be able to direct you to help.

✔ **reality check** Every year approximately 2 million teenagers attempt suicide. That's nearly fifty-five hundred a day!

Word *from the* **Word**

The Lord is close to the brokenhearted; he rescues those who are crushed in spirit. (Psalm 34:18)

You must be compassionate, just as your Father is compassionate. (Luke 6:36)

DIGGING DEEPER: *1 Samuel 31:1-4; 2 Samuel 1:6-9; 1 Kings 19:3-4*

On the Horizon

Q: How can I know God's will?

A: Trying to figure out what God wants for your life is always a challenge. God won't drop a brick out of heaven with a note attached to it telling you exactly what to do. So how can you know what God wants for your life?

First, study the Bible. This is the closest thing we have to a "note" from God. You can't know God's will if you ignore Scripture. If you want to know God's will, read his Word. The Bible may not tell you which college to attend or what career to pursue, but it will give you principles and guidelines that will help you make the right decisions.

Second, ask the advice of people you respect and who know you well. Listen to your parents, teachers, counselors, and friends who care about you and may be able to give you the guidance and direction you need. God sometimes speaks to us through other people.

Third, stay close to God. If you do your best to stay spiritually fit by praying, going to church, and being obedient to God's Word, it will be much easier to sense his direction in your life. When you are far away from God, you will find it very difficult to hear the "gentle whisper" (1 Kings 19:12) that can help you make the right choices.

Remember that God is not hiding his will from you. God's will isn't a mystery or a complicated puzzle you have to solve. If you are seeking to obey God and do what *he* wants you to do, in most cases you can do whatever *you* want to do. That's because God has a way of causing us to want what he wants. What you want to do will be the same as what he wants you to do (Philippians 2:13).

✔ reality check

Paper or plastic? White or wheat? Soccer or baseball? Piano or violin? College or tech school? Dating or just being friends? Getting a summer job or just having fun?

Our world is so full of good *things* that we feel we need God's help just to sort through them all. We worry and fret about life's options that we have, when in fact, the ability to choose is one of God's gifts to us! He will faithfully guide you back from a wrong direction if you ask him to.

God's will is that you learn to love him and become more like him. God will use all areas of your life to help fulfill his will in you. That is a pretty big job, but he's up to it!

Word
from the
Word

Keep on asking, and you will be given what you ask for. Keep on looking, and you will find. Keep on knocking, and the door will be opened. (Matthew 7:7)

DIGGING DEEPER: *Proverbs 3:5-6; Mark 4:24-25; Colossians 1:9*

#37

Q: **I have no idea what I'm going to do with my life. Nothing seems to interest me. What should I do?**

A: Don't worry too much about not knowing what you want to do with your life. Most young people don't. A hundred years ago it was a lot easier for kids to know what they were going to do because they had very few options. They usually just did whatever their parents did. If their parents were farmers, they became farmers. If their parents were doctors, they also became doctors. But today, life isn't that simple, and the choices are almost unlimited.

You don't have to make a lifetime decision right now. It will be helpful to broaden your knowledge and experience in order to learn more about yourself and what you like. And, generally speaking, as you get older you will discover and develop more interests.

If nothing seems to interest you, ask yourself some questions: "What do I like to do?" or "What am I good at?" If you like to draw pictures, you may have an aptitude for art. If you enjoy going on-line with your computer, you may want to consider a computer-related occupation. Most successful people do what they like to do and what they are good at. And everybody is good at something.

If you have trouble identifying your gifts, talents, and abilities, ask people who know you well. For example, someone might surprise you by saying, "You are a great listener. Nobody listens to me like you do." That may open the door to a career in counseling, teaching, or the ministry. Your parents would be a good place to start; a teacher, youth leader, or a friend can be helpful as well.

As you consider your interests and abilities and seek helpful advice, ask God to guide you in each step. "Trust in the Lord with all your heart; do not depend on your own understanding. Seek his will in all you do, and he will direct your paths" (Proverbs 3:5-6).

✔ reality check
"Take your mind out every now and then and dance on it. It is getting caked up." (Mark Twain, humorist and author)

Nothing interests you? Don't settle into a "case closed" way of thinking! Just because you're not interested in the same thing as your friends doesn't mean there's something wrong. Try something totally new, where your friends are not involved. Check out the offerings at the local park district. Investigate courses that are open to the community at a local college. Become an umpire. Build a radio. Interview someone you admire. Learn to repair video players. Become your youth group's official photographer. Keep a diary. Get moving!

In the words of the master of profound advice: "If you don't know where you're going, you'll wind up somewhere else." (Yogi Berra, baseball great)

Word
from the
Word

The Lord says, "I will guide you along the best pathway for your life. I will advise you and watch over you." (Psalm 32:8)

DIGGING DEEPER: *Psalms 37:23; 143:8; Jeremiah 10:23*

#38

Q: Will God's plan always be something that I don't like?

YEAH, IT'S A TOUGH JOB, BUT IT'S JUST FOR THE WINTER, SO I THINK I CAN MANAGE.

A: Yeah, that's it. God hates you and has a terrible plan for your life. (Just kidding!)

Sometimes we think that what God wants us to do and what we want to do are always going to be different. There's some truth to that our sinful nature makes us selfish, hurtful, or irresponsible. God wants us to be different, and sometimes we don't like that. But when you become a Christian and begin to grow in your faith, your desires begin to change and become more like God's. That's what the Bible means when it says, "Let God transform you into a new person by changing the way you think" (Romans 12:2). A mature Christian likes to do what God wants even when it's not easy.

Remember that Jesus came to make our lives better, not worse (John 10:10). It's not always easy to do what God wants us to—like forgiving someone who has wronged us or giving our money or time to someone in need. Jesus said that his followers are to "take up [their] cross" as they follow him (Matthew 10:38). This may sound difficult and painful, but we can trust God that we will be happier when we do his will.

✔ **reality check**   Maybe you're suffering from the early stages of *africontiphobia* (the fear of being sent to the African continent as a missionary). Actually, we made that up, but lots of Christians have that fear. In fact, Christian recording artist Scott Wesley Brown wrote a song about it called "Please Don't Send Me to Africa." Here is a portion of it:

> Please don't send me to Africa,
> I don't think I've got what it takes.
> I'm just a man, I'm not a Tarzan.
> I don't like lions, gorillas, or snakes!
> I'll serve you here in suburbia
> In my comfortable middle-class life,
> But please don't send me out in the bush
> Where the natives are restless at night!

(Scott Wesley Brown/Phill McHugh, 1989 BMG Songs, Inc., Pamela Kay Music, River Oaks, ARR, UBP)

Following God's plan for your life will mean examining your motives and desires. It will also mean learning to love and trust God in new ways. Rest assured that if you do, God can help you to overcome even "africontiphobia."

Word *from the* **Word**

"For I know the plans I have for you," says the Lord. "They are plans for good and not for disaster, to give you a future and a hope." (Jeremiah 29:11)

DIGGING DEEPER: *Psalm 40:8; Proverbs 10:24; Philippians 2:13; 1 John 2:17*

Q: What does it mean when people say, "Jesus is coming back"? How will he come back?

- THEORY #1
ANY TIME NOW!
- THEORY #2
JUST ABOUT ANY TIME NOW!

A: When Jesus left the earth, he literally went up into the clouds and disappeared. Afterward, angels told the disciples that someday Jesus would return "just as you saw him go" (Acts 1:11). Bible scholars believe this means that Jesus will return from the heaven in such a way that people will be able to see him.

The Bible makes it clear that no one knows the exact day when Jesus will come back, which is a good reason to doubt anyone who claims to know. Jesus said that he would return when people least expect it (Matthew 24:44). The Bible even says that this will happen "like a thief in the night" (1 Thessalonians 5:2). When Jesus does come back, everyone will know that he has arrived. "Everyone will see him" (Revelation 1:7).

There are many views regarding the events leading up to and following the return of Christ, primarily because much of what the Bible says about the Second Coming is in the form of prophetic visions that don't explain everything in great detail. But most Christians agree that Christ's return could happen anytime; that is why Jesus told us to always be ready for his return. This means staying close to God and doing what is right.

Although no one knows when Jesus will return, we do know that every day brings his return closer. When he comes, it will be a wonderful day for those who love him. God will create a new heaven and a new earth, where his people will live with him forever. He will put an end to all evil, suffering, pain, and death. And his people will get to be with him and with friends and family who love Jesus. We will be happier than we can possibly imagine.

Every Christian should look forward to the wonderful day of Christ's return!

✔ reality check

I never begin my work in the morning without thinking that perhaps *he* may interrupt my work and begin his own. I am not looking for death, I am looking for *him*.
—*G. Campbell Morgan, former pastor of Westminster Chapel, London*

Word
from the
Word

Now the prize awaits me—the crown of righteousness that the Lord, the righteous Judge, will give me on that great day of his return. And the prize is not just for me but for all who eagerly look forward to his glorious return.
(2 Timothy 4:8)

DIGGING DEEPER: *Mark 13:26-27; 1 Corinthians 15:51-58; 1 Thessalonians 4:16-17*

Q: How do I know if what I want to do is what God wants me to do?

A: There really isn't a foolproof way for you to know if what you want to do is what God wants you to do, but it certainly involves a decision. You need to decide and then tell God that you want to do what *he* wants you to do, to be who *he* wants you to be. In other words, ask God to cause your will to become his.

God promises to do just that (see Philippians 2:13). If you are staying close to God (reading and studying his Word, being with other Christians at church, praying, obeying his commandments), you can trust that God will be at work in you, causing you to want to do what he wants and then giving you the power to do it.

If you seek God's will and do everything you know to do,

trusting him each day, then at the end of your life, you will have done God's will. You don't have to worry about the big picture; you need to seek God and follow him today and let *him* take care of the rest.

✔ reality check

Have you ever heard the term *analysis paralysis?* It means that a person can get so busy worrying and wondering about doing the right thing that he doesn't do *anything*.

> If you come to a fork in the road, take it.
> —*Yogi Berra, baseball great*

> People who don't take risks generally make about two big mistakes a year. People who do take risks generally make about two big mistakes a year.
> —*Peter Drucker, writer, educator, management consultant*

> God can make you anything you want to be, but you have to put everything in his hands.
> —*Mahalia Jackson, gospel singer*

As scary as it may seem, part of getting wisdom about what God has for you comes from making mistakes and learning from them. Only God knows all the answers every time!

Word *from the* **Word**

Take delight in the Lord, and he will give you your heart's desires. Commit everything you do to the Lord. Trust him, and he will help you. (Psalm 37:4-5)

DIGGING DEEPER: *Proverbs 16:3; Romans 12:1-8; James 4:3*

Q: Is it true that we are not supposed to know about our future?

I THINK THE GUY WHO WRITES THESE MUST BE BORED.

YEAH! MINE SAYS, "GET A LIFE."

MINE SAYS, "HELP, I'M BEING HELD CAPTIVE IN A FORTUNE COOKIE FACTORY."

A: There is no Scripture that specifically says we shouldn't know about our future. Because we are human beings, however, there really is no way that we can. Only God is able to know what is in the future, and he rarely reveals that information to anyone else.

Some people try hard to see into the future, even consulting fortune-tellers, astrologers, and other self-proclaimed seers. The Bible is very clear about *not* looking for answers or advice there (see Deuteronomy 18:10; Leviticus 19:26).

In the Old Testament God gave his prophets information that allowed them to make prophecies that are still being fulfilled today. The New Testament book of Revelation also describes future events as God revealed them to the apostle John in a vision. But those are rare exceptions. We can live only one day at a time, which is as it should be. The Bible does reveal some things about the future, such as the fact that Christ will return. We also know that all people die—

that's part of being human. Nothing else about the future is sure. But we know that God is sovereign—he's in control—and he controls the future (see James 4:13-16).

If you knew the future, your life would be dramatically different. It would affect all your decisions and actions. If you knew you were going to die tomorrow, what would you do today? If you knew with certainty that you would live to be 100, how would that affect your life today? You would probably take more risks, knowing that nothing could hurt you.

Often people who are involved in psychic phenomena and want to know the future have the philosophy that the future is set. They think that if they knew what the future held, they could relax. In other words, they believe that the future steers the present. That is backward from God's way and takes us off track. The future is put in motion by what we do today. The future is created by the choices we make today.

We don't know what's going to happen in the future or where we'll be, but God does, and he has promised to be with us through it all. We can be hopeful about the future because of what Jesus has done in the past.

✔ reality check
The Psychic Network recently went bankrupt. If they knew the future, shouldn't they have been able to see that coming?

Word
from the
Word

How do you know what will happen tomorrow? For your life is like the morning fog—it's here a little while, then it's gone. What you ought to say is, "If the Lord wants us to, we will live and do this or that." (James 4:14-15)

DIGGING DEEPER: *Leviticus 20:6; Ecclesiastes 10:14; Micah 6:8; Matthew 6:34*

#42

Q: How can I know I'll find my perfect mate? Is there only one right person to be married to?

A: Finding the right person to marry is not like trying to find a needle in a haystack. In other words, God hasn't already picked out your perfect mate and hidden him or her somewhere for you to find. God can't choose your mate for you. That's your responsibility. (Many years ago, that might have been your parents' responsibility!) Scripture does not say that God has chosen one particular person for you to marry and that it's your job to find that him or her.

On the other hand, if you want a marriage that will be blessed by God, you need to seek his guidance and direction when you date or enter a close relationship with someone of the opposite sex. Remember that it's not always easy to make a good decision when you are falling in love or feeling attracted to another person. Take the time to explore your relationship and to make sure that you share common values and beliefs. Don't continue the relationship if you find that you do not agree on basic issues of faith and conduct. While the Bible doesn't tell you specifically whom to marry, it does warn against marrying unbelievers or those who hold a completely different set of values (2 Corinthians 6:14).

Because it's so hard to be objective about love and marriage, it's a good idea to ask the opinion of others—parents, friends, and other people you respect and who know you well (like your pastor). Sometimes we hear God's voice in the voices of others.

The good news is that when you do marry the person you have chosen (and who has chosen you) from all the others, you can trust that God will not only join you together (Matthew 19:6) but he will also bless your marriage and make both of you the "right mate" for each other. There should never be another as long as you both live. Marriage is for life.

✔ reality check   "I was in love with her but wasn't at all sure she was the girl I should ask to marry me. My plan was to marry a perfect person who had no peers, someone everyone could recognize as an angel.

"I discussed my problem with a friend, a senior big-man-on-campus type. His response was brusque: 'Look, if you *could* find a perfect girl, she wouldn't marry *you!*'"

(Ken Taylor in *My Life: A Guided Tour*)

Word
from the
Word

She is free to marry whomever she wishes, but this must be a marriage acceptable to the Lord.
(1 Corinthians 7:39)

DIGGING DEEPER: *Numbers 36:6; Judges 14:1-3; 2 Corinthians 6:14*

#43

Q: If you know God has everything under control, is it still OK to be disappointed?

A: You bet. It's also OK to feel angry, frustrated, confused, depressed, or plain old lousy. Feelings aren't right or wrong—they just are. Many people, situations, and experiences will disappoint us. People who aren't disappointed when things go wrong aren't spiritual—they're dead. The Bible gives plenty of examples of people who felt disappointment with God. Take the prophet Elijah, for example. He got so discouraged that he wanted to die (1 Kings 19:4). But after getting something to eat and a good night's sleep, he came to his senses and realized that things weren't nearly as bad as he had thought. And he was reminded that God was indeed in control.

The fact that God has things under control doesn't guarantee that only good things will happen. We live in a world where good and bad exist together. We'll have to wait until heaven before only good things happen. For now, we have to accept the fact that bad things happen to all people and that in spite of that, God is still in control.

God is able to take bad things that happen and turn them around so they result in good (Romans 8:28). He wants us to trust that he will do exactly that.

✔ **reality check**   Sometimes we're discouraged because we think we've seen the end of the story.

A father who was often away because of his job always brought a surprise to his boys when he returned home. On one occasion Dad arrived home empty-handed, leaving the two little boys disappointed. When Dad yelled, "Get in the car, guys!" the boys began to hope for ice cream. Dad drove past the ice-cream shop. When he pulled into the mall, the boys whispered together about a movie. Dad strolled past the theater entrance, and the boys' hearts sank. Finally Dad walked up to the counter in a large sports store and told the clerk, "I'm here to pick up the bikes."

The end of *your* story hasn't been written yet. God is a loving father who can be trusted to give us the best!

Word
from the
Word

For I am overwhelmed, and you alone know the way I should turn. (Psalm 142:3)

DIGGING DEEPER: *Psalms 13:1-6; 22:1-5; Lamentations 3:1-26*

Q: What if I go to college and have a particular major but don't use it?

A: We often think education has to have some practical application, but that's not necessarily so. You might wonder why you would ever study geometry if you are planning to become, say, a musician. What good is geometry to a guitar player? Actually, the value of geometry has little to do with equations and shapes. Instead, its value is in the work that you must do in order to pass the course. You have to discipline yourself, get out of your comfort zone, think in new ways, and solve complex problems. Those are skills that you need no matter what you choose to do in life.

Much of education is like that. Sure, if you want to work with computers, you'll eventually need some specific training in computers. But don't be surprised if you get trained as a computer programmer and end up owning a hardware store. Or go to law school and become a writer of mystery novels. Or get an MBA and decide to go into youth ministry. Those kinds of things happen all the time. Times change, and people change. Also, some majors don't translate into a specific career (literature, for example) but can help prepare students for a number of possibilities.

So don't worry too much about whether you'll be able to use your major right now. Just study hard, get good training, and let God lead you into the kind of work that he wants you to do. Chances are pretty good that he'll take advantage of the education that you've received and put you in a position to use your training and skills most effectively.

✔ reality check   Things you'll learn in college that probably won't be a part of your major:

- Free food served until 10:00 is gone by 9:30.
- You can know everything and fail a test.
- You can know nothing and ace a test.
- College kids throw paper airplanes too.
- If you wear polyester, everyone will ask you why you're so dressed up.
- Home is a great place to visit.
- It's possible to feel alone even when you are surrounded by friends.
- Your parents will probably seem much smarter in just a couple of years.

Word *from the* **Word**

But Amos replied, "I'm not one of your professional prophets. I certainly never trained to be one. I'm just a shepherd, and I take care of fig trees." (Amos 7:14)

DIGGING DEEPER: *1 Samuel 16:1-12; Proverbs 19:21; Philippians 3:4-8*

Q: When you die, what happens? Do you go straight to heaven?

A: Several books have been written in recent years describing the near-death experiences of people who were close to dying, but none of these books shed any real light on what actually happens when a person dies. Since no one in modern times has actually died and lived to tell about it, we can go only on what the Bible teaches.

The Bible teaches that "each person dies only once and after that comes judgment" (Hebrews 9:27). Jesus promised the dying thief on the cross, "I assure you, today you will be with me in paradise" (Luke 23:43). The Bible also says that when we are away from our bodies, "we will be at home with the Lord" (2 Corinthians 5:8). Clearly, then, when believers die, they go directly to be with Christ, and he is in heaven.

The first step in becoming a believer in Christ involves admitting to God that you are a sinner, deserving the punishment

Christ took upon himself. In other words, you have turned your back on him and have lived for yourself. The next step is to thank God for sending his Son, Jesus, to die on the cross in your place, to pay the penalty for your sin. The third step is to ask Christ to come into your life and take over—give yourself to him, no strings attached. When you do that, when you sincerely pray that prayer, God enters your life, through the Holy Spirit, and changes you into a new person (2 Corinthians 5:17). With Christ as your Savior, you can be assured that you will go to heaven when you die.

✔ **reality check** Have you ever noticed that most people who claim to believe in "previous lives" usually tell of experiences as famous historical figures? That's understandable— the stories would be a lot less interesting if they were about an unknown pig farmer in the fourth century.

There are lots of weird ideas about what happens after we die. Contrary to what many people believe, we're *not* doomed to

- keep showing up in haunted houses on Halloween;
- make surprise guest appearances at séances;
- try it all again and again and again and *again* until we get it right;
- go into some holding pen (purgatory) until our sins are paid off.

(From *Hot Topics, Tough Questions* by Bill Myers, p. 86)

Christians know that when they die, they will go immediately to be with Jesus for all eternity!

Word *from the* **Word**

Yes, we are fully confident, and we would rather be away from these bodies, for then we will be at home with the Lord. (2 Corinthians 5:8)

DIGGING DEEPER: *Luke 23:40-43; 2 Corinthians 5:10; 1 Thessalonians 4:13-14*

Q: When I look at how adults have messed up the world, I get pretty discouraged. Am I destined to become just like them?

A: Not all adults are alike, and not all adults have "messed up the world." The world could be a lot more messed up than it is. During the time of Noah, the world was so wicked that God destroyed it with the Flood. In Abraham's time, the wickedness of the people in the cities of Sodom and Gomorrah caused God to wipe them out.

Yes, the world has been messed up by adults (and by a few kids, too), but not everyone is part of the problem. (Righteous Noah and his family were saved in the ark.) Some people are working hard to "unmess up" the world, that is, to make things better. You can choose to be part of the problem or part of the solution. In fact, that's why God put the church on earth—to be salt and light, doing good, demonstrating the love of God throughout the whole world.

You can be different from those who are messing up the world; you can make a positive difference.

✔ **reality check** Our attitude tells us what to expect from life. If our "nose" is pointed up, we're taking off; if it is pointed down, we may be headed for a crash. . . .

Grandpa and Grandma had come to visit the grandchildren. Each afternoon Grandpa would lie down for a nap. One day, as a practical joke, the kids decided to put Limburger cheese in his moustache. Quite soon Grandpa awoke sniffing. "This room stinks!" he exclaimed as he left for the kitchen. He wasn't there long until he decided that the kitchen smelled too, so he went outdoors for a breath of fresh air. Much to Grandpa's surprise, the open air brought no relief, and he announced, "The whole world stinks!"

If you feel bad about your world, you'll get only negative feedback from life.

(From *The Winning Attitude* by John Maxwell, pp. 26–27)

Word *from the* **Word**

Your attitude should be the same that Christ Jesus had. (Philippians 2:5)

DIGGING DEEPER: *Genesis 6:8-18; Philippians 1:20; Psalm 81:10-13*

Q: Should Christians be involved in protecting the environment for future generations if Jesus is coming back soon anyway?

A: Christians believe that God created the heavens and the earth and declared everything that he created to be good. He also put human beings in charge of caring for the earth (Genesis 1:26). We also believe that God wants to restore the heavens and the earth, to make them new again (Romans 8:19-21), and that we can see God in his marvelous creation (Psalm 148). God loves beauty and wants us to be involved in making his world beautiful. Christians should be holy environmentalists, motivated by a strong love for God and a desire to please him in all things.

Yes, Jesus is coming back, but we don't know when. It

could be soon, or it could take another two thousand years. When Jesus does return, he wants to find us living as he taught us to live. This includes taking care of the environment, using well the resources God has entrusted to us, and preparing responsibly for the future.

If we Christians exploit the earth's resources selfishly—not caring about future generations—then we are not living as Jesus taught us to live. Think of it this way: If you knew that Jesus was coming back tomorrow, wouldn't that motivate you to be even *more* involved in doing good?

✔ **reality check** Fortunately, the condition of the environment has improved in recent years through education, recycling, and the conservation of resources. As good citizens we should continue to reduce pollution and work to improve the beauty of our planet.

But don't get "religious" on me. Some environmental groups would have you believe that the earth is our "mother" and that we should worship her! The Bible is clear that worship belongs to the Creator, not to the creation.

In truth, the earth is a lot tougher than some might think. A few years ago a single eruption of Mount Pinatubo in the Philippines spewed more ozone-depleting substances into our atmosphere than all the world's corporations had up to that time. If you think about it, volcanoes have been erupting for a long, long time. It's good to know who's been in charge of that.

Word
from the
Word

The Lord God placed the man in the Garden of Eden to tend and care for it. (Genesis 2:15)

DIGGING DEEPER: *Deuteronomy 20:19; Psalm 148:5-10; Jeremiah 12:10-11*

Q: Will God love me more if I do everything right instead of messing up all the time?

A: No. This is one big difference between Christianity and all other religions. We believe that there is nothing you can do to make God love you more than he already does. Likewise, there is nothing you can do to make God love you less. His love is complete, infinite, and never ending. God loves you so much that he sent his Son to die for you (John 3:16-17. You can go to heaven when you die if you trust in Christ as your Savior.

So does that mean you shouldn't even *try* to live right? Of course not. Nobody can avoid messing up at least some of the time, but God loves us anyway. Remember, however, that there's a big difference between acceptance and approval. Although God accepts and loves all people, he certainly doesn't approve of all they do; in fact, he *hates* many of their actions. And he allows people to experience the results of their bad choices and disobedience, including his correction (see Proverbs 3:11-12).

We should try to live right, not because God will love us more, but because we want to please God and love him more. We show God that we love him by obeying him.

✔ **reality check** In his book *Friends Are Friends Forever*, Michael W. Smith talks about not feeling good enough for God and gives his own paraphrase of Psalm 103:10-12:

> God is nuts about us. This psalm goes on to say that God has compassion for us the way that a father has compassion for his children. That analogy is powerful to a dad like me.
>
> I am crazy about my kids, but sometimes they do things that try my patience. Yet even in their worst moments of tantrum throwing or stubbornness, I still love them. When they feel left out by their classmates or fail in something they try, it really wears me out too. Over the past few years, God has been calling me to be a better father, but I know that my level of compassion does not approach how much He cares for us.

(From *Friends Are Friends Forever and Other Encouragements from God's Word*, Thomas Nelson Publishers, 1997, pp. 36–37)

Word *from the* **Word**

The Lord is like a father to his children, tender and compassionate to those who fear him. For he understands how weak we are; he knows we are only dust. (Psalm 103:13-14)

DIGGING DEEPER: *Psalm 103:1-18; Ephesians 4:30-32*

Q: **Most of the time I wish I were someone else. Why did God make me this way?**

A: It's all right to wish you were *like* someone else. Sometimes that can help you become all that God created you to be. It's good to have heroes, people to look up to, to want to be like. Hopefully you can find heroes or role models who have positive qualities that you want to develop in your own life.

On the other hand, it's wrong to wish you were someone else simply because that person is good looking or rich or has something that you don't have. One of the Ten Commandments warns against covetousness, that is, wanting what somebody else has. When you covet, you grow more and more unhappy with what you have. That leads to low self-esteem and sometimes self-destructive behaviors.

God doesn't make junk. Every single human being was created in God's image, including you. But because of evil in the world, God's creation is marred, or spoiled. Sometimes children are born with physical handicaps or into poverty or abusive families. Despite your circumstances, however, you can be all that God created you to be. The secret to a happy life is much more than having money, a high IQ, or good looks.

God gave you feelings and the opportunity to think and choose. It's easy to compare yourself to others. Instead of wishing to be someone else, however, thank God for making you the way you are. Look for the good he created in you, and look for ways you can use your God-given talents and abilities for good.

✔ reality check

Christian recording artist Kathy Troccoli used to feel the same way. "I've had struggles and insecurities all my life. It's taken me a long time to learn to really love and accept myself. I didn't know what I wanted out of life. I didn't like myself too much. I was . . . caring too much about what other people thought. You know—*Do they like me? And if they don't, am I OK?* I know what that feels like—to not feel good about yourself, to be intimidated by someone else."

What is her advice? "I believe if you really take God at His Word, you'll realize that you can become a beautiful soul because Jesus lives inside you. . . . That means we can acquire some of His characteristics. For me, that alone causes this unbelievable confidence when I walk into a room. He has made all the difference in me. You can't muster that up—and if you try, it's going to be from some of those tangible things that won't last."

(From *Brio* magazine, published by Focus on the Family, 8, no. 10, October 1997, pp. 18–21)

Word
from the
Word

Enjoy what you have rather than desiring what you don't have. Just dreaming about nice things is meaningless; it is like chasing the wind.
(Ecclesiastes 6:9)

DIGGING DEEPER: *Exodus 20:17; Psalm 73:1-24; James 3:14-16*

Q: How can I figure out what I'm good at?

A: What do you like to do? You may be surprised that even some of the fun activities you enjoy are clues that can lead you to a lifelong career. For example, if you enjoy doodling during class, that could mean that you have talent in art or that you are a creative thinker and might do well as a business entrepreneur. If you like to talk a lot, you might have a talent for teaching, public speaking, or sales. If you enjoy sports, you might consider athletics, coaching, or some aspect of the sports business. If you enjoy solving puzzles, you might be a good lawyer or even an archaeologist.

Another way to learn what you're good at is to ask people who know you well. Sometimes your parents, friends, teachers, and youth pastor will be able to identify gifts and abilities in you that you never realized you had.

Another possibility is to take a specialized test. It will ask you lots of questions about yourself and then give you a report on your aptitudes and abilities and the kinds of careers that might fit you best.

Perhaps the best way to find out what you're good at is to get involved in some kind of ministry. Go on a mission trip, help out with the youth group at church, or join a club at school that is service oriented. When you are doing something positive, you often are in the best position to discover your gifts and to receive affirmation from others.

God has given every person a variety of gifts and abilities for the purpose of serving him and making a difference in the world. Some of these gifts are listed in 1 Corinthians 12, Romans 12, and Ephesians 4 in the Bible. Every Christian is responsible for identifying his or her gifts and then using them! Discovering and using one's gifts can help a person discover God's plan for his or her life. God has created each person as a unique individual, and he has a plan for each person that matches his or her gifts and abilities.

✔ **reality check**   Don't you hate it when people give you the same stale advice? "Keep your eyes on the ball, your shoulder to the wheel, your ear to the ground, and your nose to the grindstone."

If you can do *anything* in *that* position, you don't need anybody's advice!

Word
from the
Word

God has given each of us the ability to do certain things well. . . . If your gift is that of serving others, serve them well. If you are a teacher, do a good job of teaching. (Romans 12:6-7)

DIGGING DEEPER: *Genesis 39:2-6; 41:37-41; Acts 6:2-3*

Q: **I seem to act differently with different groups of kids. How can I tell which me is the real me?**

Athletic Friends | Music Friends | Academic Friends | Playing With My Cat

A: If you have a problem with being consistent, you are not alone. It's natural to try on different roles to see which one is you. Eventually you'll settle in. So relax, but don't fit in by doing what is wrong. It's very easy to be like a chameleon, the lizard that changes color to match its surroundings. It's important to avoid surroundings that can get you into trouble. If you are with a group of kids who are involved in behaviors that you know are wrong, the best thing to do is leave.

Remember that the real you is the you that God created you to be. And the best way to remember who you really are is to stay close to God. When you are far away from God, it's a lot easier to forget who you are and to be swayed and influenced by the world. That's one of the reasons why it's important to have a daily time with God, reading his Word and praying, so that you will be reminded every day that you are a child of God, created to bring honor and glory to him. Then, when you are tempted to act differently, you will have the strength to be the real you.

✔ **reality check**   One of Aesop's fables describes a war between the animals and the birds. The bat was unsure about which group to fight for, so he tried to belong to both camps. When the birds scored a victory, the bat would fly around and brag about the power of the birds. But when the direction of the war changed and the animals started to win, the bat walked into the animal camp to promise loyalty. His two-faced strategy failed, and the bat was rejected by both groups. The angry groups agreed on one thing— that the bat had better run for its life! That is why it comes out only at night.

Just like the bat, you probably have things in common with several groups. You won't fit in with every group for very long. Most likely, you already know who the "real me" should be. Ask God to help you choose wisely. Sooner or later, one side will win.

Word
from the
Word

Don't copy the behavior and customs of this world, but let God transform you into a new person by changing the way you think. (Romans 12:2)

DIGGING DEEPER: *Proverbs 25:26; Ephesians 2:10; Colossians 1:9-10*

Q: How do you define a "bad" person?

A: Actually, every person is "bad," and every person is "good." All of us are bad because we are all sinners. The Bible doesn't make a distinction between bad people and good people. Instead, the Bible says that "all have sinned; all fall short of God's glorious standard" (Romans 3:23). This means that every person has a basic sin nature—everyone does wrong naturally.

At the same time, however, every person is good because all people have been created by God, in his image. God sees his human creatures as good. Even though we sin greatly, God loves us—to the point of sending his Son to die for us. Had God decided that we were all totally bad and worthless, beyond hope, he would simply have destroyed us all and not sent Jesus to die to save us.

Those who trust in Christ—accept him as their personal Savior—are forgiven their sins and are given the power to be and do good. God expects his people to spend their lives doing good.

When Jesus was crucified, he said to one of the criminals next to him, "I assure you, today you will be with me in paradise" (Luke 23:43). During World War II a German pastor was asked what he would say to Adolf Hitler if he had the opportunity. He replied, "Jesus Christ died for your sins." That is the message of the gospel.

No person is beyond the grace of God. Even the worst offenders can be restored to "goodness" if they will just accept the love of God and turn from their sins. Thankfully, that includes all of us.

✔ reality check

He had the hardest face you've ever seen. His mother had nicknamed him "son of Satan" as part of her practice of witchcraft. At eighteen he was the leader of a powerful street gang skilled at robbery, intimidation, violence, and drugs. When the preacher offered a handshake, the young man replied: "You come near me, I'll kill you."

He may sound like just another "bad" guy from a street gang, but this story began forty years ago. The man's name is Nicky Cruz. The preacher is David Wilkerson. Though few believed these vicious street punks were worth the effort, Nicky was changed by God's love. Both Nicky and David continue to spend their lives with people who are desperate for the good news of Christ. They have worked to support drug-rehabilitation centers, job-training programs, an AIDS hospital, and antigang programs.

To get the full story, read *The Cross and the Switchblade* by David Wilkerson.

Word
from the
Word

There is not a single person in all the earth who is always good and never sins. (Ecclesiastes 7:20)

DIGGING DEEPER: *Isaiah 64:5-6; Romans 3:22-23; 1 John 1:8-9*

#53

Q: People tell me I'm a loser. Why shouldn't I believe them?

A: There was once a little boy the other children called Sparky, after a comic-strip horse named Sparkplug.

School was difficult for Sparky. He failed every subject in the eighth grade. He flunked physics in high school. He also flunked Latin, algebra, and English. He didn't do much better in sports. He made the school's golf team, but his poor play cost his team the championship.

Sparky did have a hobby. He loved cartoons, and he liked drawing his own cartoons.

He dreamed about being an artist for Walt Disney. So after graduating from high school, he wrote a letter to the Walt Disney studios inquiring about job opportunities. He received a form letter asking him to draw a funny cartoon of "a man repairing a clock by shoveling the springs and gears back inside it."

Sparky drew the cartoon and mailed it and some of his other artwork off to the Disney studios. He waited and waited for a reply. Finally the reply came—another form letter explaining that there was no job for him.

Sparky was disappointed but not surprised. He had always been a loser, and this was just one more loss. He thought his life was kind of funny in a weird sort of way. So he wrote his own life story in cartoons. He described his childhood—the misadventures of a little boy loser, the chronic underachiever—in a cartoon that has become known worldwide.

The young artist who failed the eighth grade was "Sparky" Charles Monroe Schultz—creator of the "Peanuts" comic strip. And the little boy loser whose kite would never fly? Charlie Brown.

The final chapters of your life have not been written. The game is only in the first quarter so don't give up on yourself. Remember that God is in control of your life, not those who want to put you down. God says you're a winner. Only what God thinks truly matters.

✔ reality check

Beethoven can write music, thank God—but he can do nothing else on earth.
—*Beethoven*

But Lord, . . . how can I rescue Israel? My clan is the weakest in the whole tribe of Manasseh, and I am the least in my entire family!
—*Gideon, Judges 6:15 (Read Judges 7–8 for the full story!)*

Why shouldn't you believe what people tell you? Because God proves people wrong all the time.

Word
from the
Word

God chose things despised by the world, things counted as nothing at all, and used them to bring to nothing what the world considers important. (1 Corinthians 1:28)

DIGGING DEEPER: *Isaiah 53:2-3; Luke 18:9-14; 1 Corinthians 1:26-29; 2 Corinthians 3:5*

Q: **Is it acceptable to change your appearance with plastic surgery, tattoos, body piercing, etc.?**

A: Certainly some plastic surgery may be necessary to correct a deformity or to help a person after a terrible accident. But much of plastic surgery is solely to try to enhance a person's looks. The Bible doesn't prohibit this stuff, but why do it?

These days, many kids change their appearance simply because they want to be like the crowd or like popular rock stars or celebrities. Maybe teens want to be different, make a statement, or project a certain image. But it is never wise to simply imitate the crowd. A herd mentality causes people to do things they would never do if they were acting alone. So first, make sure that the crowd with whom you want to identify will build you up, not drag you down.

Second, remember that fads come and go. Changing your appearance is often permanent. Tattoos definitely are. Body piercing can result in serious health problems. Many adults deeply regret what they did to their bodies when they were teenagers. Be careful, and always make sure that your parents will allow whatever you choose to do.

It's all right to improve your appearance, but don't do something that you will regret later. Your body is changing rapidly during your teen years, and God isn't finished with you. The real you is what is on the inside. The most important people in your life won't care about the outside, but they will care a lot about what's in your heart.

✔ reality check   Here are some things that people in the past have done to improve their appearance:

- Greeks in the time of Alexander the Great liked the blond hair that is fashionable today. They created the reddish blond color using potash water and herbs.
- In 1400 B.C. it was high style among wealthy Egyptian women to wear large cones of scented grease on top of their heads. As the day passed, the grease would melt and drip over their skin and clothing to release the perfume.
- Eighteenth-century Englishmen wore their pants so tight that the pants were hung on special pegs so the men could jump down into them.
- Fashionable women in medieval Japan blackened their teeth.
- The Mayan Indians filed their front teeth to points, drilled holes in them, and either filled them or hung precious gems from them.

(From *2201 Fascinating Facts* by David Louis)

Word *from the* **Word**

People judge by outward appearance, but the Lord looks at a person's thoughts and intentions. (1 Samuel 16:7)

DIGGING DEEPER: *Leviticus 19:28; 1 Timothy 2:9-10; 1 Peter 3:3-4*

#55

Q: **If drugs make me feel so good, why shouldn't I take them?**

A: It's not sinful to feel good, but good feelings are not the ultimate good—pleasing God is.

There's a story about a man who jumped off the Empire State Building because he really liked the feeling of falling unrestricted through the air with the wind blowing through his hair. On the way down, someone heard him saying, "This is terrific! I've never felt so wonderful!" Of course, a short time later he never felt so dead.

Drugs are a lot like that. They make you feel good for a short time, but then they drop you like a rock. Every drug addict will tell you the same thing. The temporary euphoria that comes from doing drugs isn't worth what comes later. If drugs don't kill you, they will ruin your health, destroy your self-esteem, ruin your relationships, prevent you from achieving happiness or success in life, and possibly even get you a prison sentence. In short, drugs cost too much.

Taking drugs is wrong because it's against the law and because drugs harm both body and mind. People who use drugs often harm others, too.

If you are Christian, there are other important issues to consider. When you are on drugs, for example, you are letting a foreign substance control your life. The Bible says that we should be under the control of the Spirit of God, not under the control of drugs or alcohol (Ephesians 5:18). "Don't you know that your body is the temple of the Holy Spirit, who lives in you and was given to you by God? You do not belong to yourself" (1 Corinthians 6:19). Your body belongs to God and is where his Holy Spirit dwells. As Christians, therefore, we should do everything we can to stay healthy and physically fit.

God is not against feeling good. In fact, he wants us to feel the very best we can. And if we are living our lives according to his plan for us, we will. God doesn't tell us to do or not do certain things because he doesn't want us to have fun but because he loves us, knows what is best for us, and wants only the best for us.

✔ reality check
Use of drugs generally results in a huge increase in the "duh" factor. Read on. . . .

A man in Pontiac, Michigan, who was arrested on drug-possession charges claimed to have been searched without a warrant. The prosecutor in the case noted that the officer didn't need a warrant because a "bulge" in the suspect's pocket could have been a weapon.

"No way!" responded the defendant. Since he happened to be wearing the same jacket that day in court, he removed it and handed it to the judge to examine. The judge discovered a packet of cocaine in the pocket! A five-minute recess was required in order for the judge to stop laughing.

Word *from the* **Word**

Don't you realize that all of you together are the temple of God and that the Spirit of God lives in you? God will bring ruin upon anyone who ruins this temple. For God's temple is holy, and you Christians are that temple. (1 Corinthians 3:16-17)

DIGGING DEEPER: *Proverbs 6:27-28; 14:12; 1 John 2:15-17*

#56

Q: Why do I always seem to need more money?

A: People never feel they have enough money; they always want more because money doesn't satisfy. Money can be like a drug, and people can become obsessed with getting rich. It's hard to believe, but many of the richest people on earth think they need more money. In fact, the more money you have, the more money you tend to want. If you have enough money to buy a new CD player, then you want more money to buy new CDs. If you have enough money to buy a new pair of shoes, then you want more money to buy a matching outfit. If you have enough money to buy a house, then you want more money to decorate it, fix it up, furnish it, and pay all the utilities and taxes. If you have enough money to buy an expensive car, then you want more money to pay for repair bills and higher insurance rates. And on it goes. If you're not careful, you can end up on a treadmill, working harder and spending more but enjoying life a lot less.

Some people need money more than others because they don't carefully manage what they have. That's why you must learn to set spending limits for yourself and then live within those limits. It's helpful to differentiate between needs and wants. You don't always *need* what you *want*. The world tries to make you think you need more than you do—to make you want more than you need. But if you can learn to live within your means and budget your money wisely, you will learn one of the secrets to a happy life—being content with what you have (see Philippians 4:11-12). If you can learn to be content and responsible with what you have, even if it's only a little, God may trust you to handle more (see Matthew 25:21).

✔ reality check   Here's a guy who could have used a little less money. . . .

A thirty-three-year-old man was recently arrested in Providence, Rhode Island, after allegedly knocking out an armored-car driver and stealing the closest four bags of money. As it turned out, the bags contained eight hundred dollars in pennies and weighed thirty pounds each. As the thief tried to run away, he was soon slowed to a stagger, and police easily caught him from behind.

Word *from the* **Word**

Don't weary yourself trying to get rich. Why waste your time? For riches can disappear as though they had the wings of a bird! (Proverbs 23:4-5)

DIGGING DEEPER: *Ecclesiastes 5:10-12; Philippians 4:11-12; 1 Timothy 6:6-10*

Q: **Is it OK to have a part-time job during the school year?**

A: There's nothing wrong with having a part-time job during the school year. Before getting one, however, ask yourself these questions:

1. Will my job interfere with school? Will it cause me to be late or so tired that I can't stay awake in class? or to not have enough time to do my homework?
2. Will my job prevent me from participating in other activities, like going out for sports, being a leader at school, getting involved in my church youth group, or spending time with my family?
3. Will my job help me grow as a person? Will I learn important skills and abilities? Is it a job that I can be proud of?
4. Why do I want this job? Is it merely to make money so I can buy more stuff? Or am I interested in doing something worthwhile with my spare time, contributing to my family, or learning a skill that I can use later in life?

Remember, a student's main job is to be a student. In most cases, being a student is a full-time occupation. It requires a lot of time and effort in order to be successful. If you really don't need the money or if working part-time isn't absolutely necessary, then it's usually best to concentrate on your schoolwork and avoid the pressure that a job will put on your time and your life.

✔ reality check If you're really interested in a job, here's a list of things *not* to do in your interview:

- Dress for Less: Wear your favorite torn T-shirt and your mowing shoes.
- Speed Is the Key: Don't sweat issues like spelling and hand-writing on the application—just finish.
- The More the Merrier: Bring a friend along for moral support during the interview.
- Be a Bud: Remember, that interviewer is just a person, like you. Drop the "ma'am" or "sir" routine.
- Take Over the Company: Give plenty of suggestions for improving the company.
- Wail Your Woes: Fill the interviewer in on everything you hated about your last job.

(Adapted from "How to Lose Out on a Really Great Job" by Sharon Wilharm, *Brio* magazine, June 1997)

Word
from the
Word

Being wise is as good as being rich; in fact, it is better. Wisdom or money can get you almost anything, but it's important to know that only wisdom can save your life. (Ecclesiastes 7:11-12)

DIGGING DEEPER: *Numbers 11:4-6; Ecclesiastes 9:10; 11:6*

Q: **Is money itself bad (evil)?**

A: No, not at all. Money can be wonderful when it is used to do good. The Bible does say, however, that the *love* of money is "at the root of all kinds of evil" (1 Timothy 6:10). That's because it leads to idolatry; money becomes some people's god. They worship it. Their lives are controlled by it, and all their decisions are based on it. People who love money more than they love God wind up not only separated from God but also terribly unhappy.

Like everything good, money is a gift from God (James 1:17). He wants us to be thankful for money and to use it wisely. Jesus told the parable of the talents to teach that we should use what God gives us to accomplish great things for the kingdom of God (Matthew 25:15-28). There's nothing wrong with working hard to earn money, as long as earning money is not our ultimate purpose in life. Our purpose in life should be to glorify God and serve him. When we do that, the money we earn can be used not only to buy the things *we* need but also to bless the lives of others who are in need.

✔ **reality check** Every day millions of people take a medicine that is necessary for them to stay alive. This medicine is for patients who have already had or are in danger of having a stroke. It thins the blood to make it less likely that a blockage will form. The active ingredient in this medicine is the same substance used in another common compound—rat poison. Is this medicine bad? Just as with money, it all depends on how it is used.

Think of five everyday needs that are met with money. Think of five luxuries you could have spent money on this week. Think of five bad or hurtful things that money can be used for. Think of five ways that money could be used to help other people.

Think of one way you could improve your use of money this week.

Word from the Word

For the love of money is at the root of all kinds of evil. And some people, craving money, have wandered from the faith and pierced themselves with many sorrows. (1 Timothy 6:10)

DIGGING DEEPER: *Psalm 62:10; Matthew 6:24; 1 Timothy 6:9*

#59

Q: Is it wrong to desire to live in a big house, have a nice car, and have expensive things?

A: That may be wrong for some people. For example, it would be wrong to want those things simply to impress others or to achieve status. The world may be impressed with people who look wealthy and have expensive things, but God isn't impressed at all. God cares about what a person has on the inside, not what's on the outside (1 Samuel 16:7). A person with godly values doesn't care what the world thinks but what God thinks.

It would also be wrong to want those things, knowing that if you bought them, you wouldn't be able to give money to help the poor or to support the ministries of the church. If God has blessed you with enough money to live in a big house, then he has probably blessed you with enough money to help others. If you spend all your money on yourself, it's unlikely that you are being a responsible follower of Jesus Christ.

There is nothing inherently wrong with having big, nice, or expensive things, but money and possessions don't bring lasting happiness and fulfillment. In fact, they often bring worry (Matthew 6:31-34).

Perhaps a good rule of thumb is to seek to serve God as effectively as you can wherever God has put you. A business executive probably will be more effective with a nice car and nice clothes than with an old, beat-up car and faded blue jeans. On the other hand, the reverse would be true for someone serving the poor in Calcutta, as Mother Teresa did. God isn't that concerned about what you have or don't have. He is interested in whether or not you are serving him and putting him first in everything. If you are doing that, you will make good decisions about how to spend your money.

✔ **reality check**   Here are questions that could help you judge your desire for more "stuff":

- Could I rent, borrow, or co-own this thing instead of buying it?
- Is this the most efficient, most durable model I can buy?
- Instead of buying this, could I repair or modify something I already have?
- Will this purchase make me less likely to serve Jesus in the next five years?

(Adapted from *The Christian Book of Lists* by Randy Petersen, p. 176)

Remember, the one who dies with the most toys . . . still dies.

Word
from the
Word

Beware! Don't be greedy for what you don't have. Real life is not measured by how much we own. (Luke 12:15)

DIGGING DEEPER: *Deuteronomy 8:11-14; Job 1:1-31; 1 Timothy 6:6-10, 17-19*

Q: Why is the church always asking for money?

A: It is part of God's plan for Christians to give money to the church so the church can do God's work and help others learn how to follow him. Like families and businesses, churches have bills to pay. Churches also have to pay salaries to the pastors and secretaries. The church's money pays for ministries such as Sunday school, missions, youth groups, and special events. Churches don't sell tickets for the worship services or sell products, so they get their money from people in the congregation who give freely.

One of the ways we thank God for what he has given us is by giving a portion back to him. We put money in the offering plate not just to help the church pay its bills but because we love God. We love God because he first loved us. We give to him because he has given to us. Every church provides its members an opportunity to give. That's what a church is supposed to do.

When church leaders ask for money, it is rarely because the church is greedy or trying to get rich. They are simply reminding people that giving is part of their responsibility as Christians. And sometimes the church is informing people of new opportunities to give to worthy causes, such as to help the poor, support missionaries, or do something important, like build a new place of worship.

✔ **reality check** Why does your all-out, four-star, room-cleaning job last only a week at best? Why do some students begin the school year with "zip" and end with "zero"? Why do many people begin three or four diets a year?

Because *making* a commitment is easier than *keeping* one. Deep down, most Christians want to be faithful in giving to their church. But we lose steam pretty easily, don't we? God knows that we need encouragement—a push now and then—to keep our commitments. Try taking notes and summarizing the sermon in your church service for three months. You may find out that money isn't the only topic that gets your attention!

Word from the Word

Don't you know that those who work in the Temple get their meals from the food brought to the Temple as offerings? And those who serve at the altar get a share of the sacrificial offerings. In the same way, the Lord gave orders that those who preach the Good News should be supported by those who benefit from it. (1 Corinthians 9:13-14)

DIGGING DEEPER: *Malachi 3:10; 2 Corinthians 9:11-12; 1 Timothy 5:17-18*

#61

Q: How much money should I give to the offering?

A: It's completely up to you. In Old Testament times, the law God gave to Moses set the tithe (10 percent) as the standard for giving, but in the New Testament we are instructed to give generously from our hearts.

Jesus taught that we should give to God because we love him and love other people. Our motivation for giving should be rooted in gratitude and compassion, not because we have to. In reality, everything we have belongs to God, so if we can give more than 10 percent, then we should do it—gladly. "God loves the person who gives cheerfully" (2 Corinthians 9:7).

Most churches teach that believers should tithe (give 10 percent) because it's good to have a starting point. But remember to give to God because you love him and want to express your love in a tangible way. God has a lot more that he wants to give you, but he can't do it if your hands are full.

✔ **reality check** Maybe you really would like to give money at church, but you can't give it if you don't have it. The best way to determine how much money to give to your church is to take a look at how you're spending your money. Get some paper and a pencil and try this exercise:

1. How much money is yours to control on a weekly basis? Allowance? Baby-sitting or other jobs? Put that amount as a beginning balance.
2. What expenses are you expected to cover with your money? School lunches? Movies? CDs? Magazines or makeup? Gifts for friends? Estimate the amount you spend weekly and subtract from your beginning balance.
3. Are you expected to save a portion of your money? How much? Subtract that amount.
4. Don't be surprised if your balance is already at zero or below. Now you know why giving to the church takes commitment and heart desire.
5. Now, determine what amount would be 10 percent of your beginning balance. Ask yourself: *Am I willing to give that amount to my church without regret?* Be honest. If you can't feel good about that amount, is there an amount you would be willing to give?
6. Once you decide on an amount, go back to your beginning total and subtract that amount *first*. You'll probably find that giving will require an adjustment in the way you spend the rest of your money.
7. One final suggestion: To help you keep track of your money going out, create envelopes marked "Church," "Save," and "Spend." Divide your money into the categories as soon as you get it, and don't borrow from "Church" and "Save" to "Spend"!

Word
from the
Word

You must each make up your own mind as to how much you should give. Don't give reluctantly or in response to pressure. For God loves the person who gives cheerfully. (2 Corinthians 9:7)

DIGGING DEEPER: *1 Chronicles 29:14; Luke 6:38; 2 Corinthians 8:1-15*

#62

Q: Should I start saving money now for when I'm old and can't work anymore?

A: It's a good idea to get into the habit of saving as early as you can. If you can learn to save a little bit of money regularly (every time you get your allowance or a paycheck), you will not only have some money for a future emergency or for when you get old, but you will also learn self-discipline and self-control in your finances.

Some people wait until they are already pretty old to start saving for retirement, but consider this: If you start saving a little now and let it grow in an investment, by the time you are old, it will probably be worth many times what you put in. The trick is letting it grow for as long as possible. You have time on your side now, even though you don't have much money. So if you can discipline yourself to save just a little on a regular basis, chances are you will have all you need for your retirement years.

When you finish your education and have a job, you may be

able to open a retirement account that will grow much faster because it isn't taxed every year.

If you are able to do it, save. Remember, however, that a Christian's security is in heaven, not in the bank. Jesus reassured his followers that God would take care of them and that it is pointless to worry about the future (Matthew 6:25-27). God is in control. Some people become obsessed with accumulating wealth because they are worried about the future, but Jesus taught that we should "store up treasure in heaven" (Luke 12:33). Those with a lot of money often worry more because they fear losing it. There's nothing wrong with saving money and planning for your retirement years, but remember that your security is not based on what *you* can do but on what *God* has promised to do. He will take care of you.

✔ **reality check** It's almost unbelievable to see what happens to a small amount of money over a long period of time. Think about this scenario. Your grandparents give you a savings account worth fifteen hundred dollars for your thirteenth birthday. You invest the money in a fund that pays 8 percent interest. Every year you add just fifty dollars to the account. By the time you retire at sixty-five, that account will be worth over one million dollars! No kidding!

To see for yourself, use the calculator on this Web site: www.worldi.com. It's interesting that the factor that changes the final total the most is the number of years saved, not the amount added each year. So get started!

Word *from the* **Word**

Take a lesson from the ants, you lazybones. Learn from their ways and be wise! Even though they have no prince, governor, or ruler to make them work, they labor hard all summer, gathering food for the winter. (Proverbs 6:6-8)

DIGGING DEEPER: *Genesis 41:35-36; Proverbs 20:4; 22:3*

#63

Q: Is gambling wrong?

HE'S LIKE THIS RIGHT AFTER HE GETS HIS ALLOWANCE!

A: Well, it's keeping baseball great Pete Rose out of the Hall of Fame.

Gambling can be very seductive. It creates the illusion that a person can get rich simply by picking the right numbers or betting on the right team. It seems so easy. But when you hear those advertisements for the lottery, you only hear about the people who win. You don't hear about the millions who lose. In fact, gambling is based on the premise that 99.9 percent of the gamblers have to *lose* in order for someone to win.

Never forget that gambling is always designed to separate you from your money. You are guaranteed to lose more than you win. That's the way gambling works. Yes, it is possible to win something once in a while, but the odds are always against you, so in the long run you will lose. The fact is that those who can *least* afford to lose usually gamble the *most*.

Does the Bible prohibit gambling? There is no specific mention of people betting on horses or football games or playing the lottery, but the Bible does offer warnings like this one: "But people who long to be rich fall into temptation and are trapped by many foolish and harmful desires that plunge them into ruin and destruction" (1 Timothy 6:9). Gambling is addictive and can destroy lives. That's why organizations like Gamblers Anonymous have sprung up.

The Bible also says that "the person who wants to get rich quick will only get into trouble" (Proverbs 28:20). Gambling interests promote this easy, get-rich-quick myth. Instead of trying to get rich "quick and easy," we need to realize that money should be earned through honest hard work.

✔ reality check   What do the following activities have in common?

- Getting married at sixteen
- Eating an entire carton of rocky road ice cream
- Hang gliding in stormy weather
- Betting your allowance in a football pool
- Petting a wild skunk
- Smoking cigarettes
- Walking alone in the city at 3:00 A.M.
- Bungee jumping with an extralong cord

People *can* do all these things, but that doesn't mean these things *should* be done! First Corinthians 6:12 says, "You may say, 'I am allowed to do anything.' But I reply, 'Not everything is good for you.' And even though, 'I am allowed to do anything,' I must not become a slave to anything."

Word
from the
Word

Lazy people want much but get little, but those who work hard will prosper and be satisfied. (Proverbs 13:4)

DIGGING DEEPER: *Proverbs 21:5; 28:20; 1 Timothy 6:8-10*

#64

Q: **What's the point of working so hard for a few lousy bucks when all the really successful people are making millions?**

A: It can be discouraging to hear about all the professional athletes and entertainers who are making huge salaries. But it's helpful to remember that the number of people who are pulling in the big bucks is very small. Only about one percent of the population is "making millions." And of those, most became millionaires by "working hard for a few lousy bucks." Most successful people got that way by working hard, working smart, and being smart with their money. Nobody just handed them their millions.

It's also helpful to remember that money is not a very good way to judge success. Many very successful people aren't millionaires, and lots of millionaires aren't very successful. In fact, quite a few of them are miserable. Over and over we hear about very rich people whose personal lives are empty, whose relationships are a disaster, and who suffer from continual stress and depression. Sometimes the world's idea of success is nothing more than a trap that can literally drive a person insane. A famous example is the multibillionaire Howard Hughes, who died an eccentric, neurotic hermit.

If you want to be successful, don't worry about money. Instead, be concerned with pleasing God. Colossians 3:23 says: "Work hard and cheerfully at whatever you do, as though you were working for the Lord rather than for people." This verse was originally written to slaves, who weren't getting paid at all! God wants you to work hard at whatever job you do and bring glory to him in the process. Follow God's plan for your life, work hard, be generous, and manage your money well, and God will take care of you! He might even let you become a millionaire!

✔ **reality check**   Three boys applied for a summer job at a hardware store. Only one position was available, but the owner hired all the boys for one day. He would decide at the end of the day which one would get the job.

When the boys arrived, the owner took them to the back and asked them to move an old pile of broken bricks to the other side of the yard. All three worked diligently to finish quickly. The owner commended them and gave them the second job. They were to transport the same bricks to their original spot. The boys thought it strange but, knowing that it was a test, set out to do the job. They finished with a lot of time left. When the owner requested that they move the bricks a third time, one boy declined to participate, saying, "Sir, I'm grateful for the opportunity, but I do not want to work at a job that has no purpose. You can choose between the other two." The owner hired that boy on the spot.

Word *from the* **Word**

Riches won't help on the day of judgment, but right living is a safeguard against death. (Proverbs 11:4)

DIGGING DEEPER: *Proverbs 15:16; Luke 12:15*

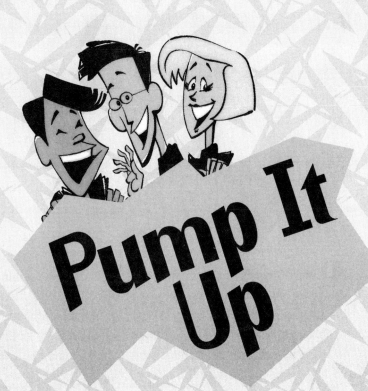

Pump It Up

#65

Q: How does music affect me?

A: Music affects you in several ways: First, it affects your emotions, your feelings. Depending on the music you're listening to, you can feel happy or sad, calm or agitated, violent, romantic, or scared. Music is a powerful emotional stimulant, which is why movie sound tracks work so well. Action movies usually have loud, fast, and frantic music. Suspense movies use eerie music that makes your skin crawl. Romantic movies will incorporate soft, classical music. When you go to church, music helps create an atmosphere of worship.

If you understand the power of music to affect your emotions, you can use music to help you feel better. Some kids wonder why they feel so stressed out all the time. It may have something to do with the music they listen to all day long. There is a definite relationship between the two.

Music affects you in other ways too. For example, music can promote values or behaviors—both good and bad. The words to some songs encourage sexual promiscuity, violence, drug

142

abuse, or involvement in the occult. Listening to that kind of music can negatively affect you. You may listen just because you like the beat or the "feeling" of the music. If it is communicating values that are in opposition to what you know is right, however, it will eventually compromise your ability to make good decisions. At the very least, it will prevent you from relaxing and enjoying the music because the words conflict with what you believe.

Music can move and motivate—the words sink in and can fill minds and influence actions. Find music that you enjoy and that doesn't conflict with who you are and what you believe.

✔ reality check   You are the director for the following
scenes from the Bible. Match the appropriate musical "effect."

1. David returns the ark of the covenant to the temple.
2. Jesus prays in the Garden of Gethsemane.
3. Adam sees Eve for the first time.
4. Paul is shipwrecked in a storm.

a. Stringed instruments playing a sweeping, romantic melody
b. Blaring horns, thundering drums, crashing symbols
c. Rhythmic dance tune with driving percussion
d. Mournful Celtic tune played in a minor key on a flute or pipe

Try this on your own. Think of a Bible event, and set it to music. Hey, maybe there's a career in this for you!

Word
from the
Word

Let us find a good musician to play the harp for you whenever the tormenting spirit is bothering you. The harp music will quiet you, and you will soon be well again. (1 Samuel 16:16)

DIGGING DEEPER: *Job 12:11; Ephesians 5:19-20; Philippians 4:8*

Q: What's the difference between regular rock and Christian rock music?

A: The main difference is that Christian rock is performed by Christians. Ditto with Christian country, Christian rap, or Christian polka music. If Christians are singing and playing it, then the music, the lyrics (words), and the presentation should be consistent with the values and beliefs of the Christian faith.

Of course, some Christian artists write and perform songs that speak directly about God, Jesus, and the Christian life. Usually those songs are called Christian, religious, or spiritual, and the others, secular. But that's a pretty artificial distinction.

There are some extremely talented Christian rock musicians on the scene today, but they often have trouble becoming successful in the secular world because they refuse to compromise their values and beliefs just to sell more records or to achieve more fame. Today's rock stars often have to be shocking in order to be popular, and that excludes some of the most gifted performers who won't play by those rules.

The best way to tell the difference between secular rock and Christian rock is to check out the lifestyles of the musicians who perform it (why they perform, how they perform, how they live, how they use the money, and so forth). That usually speaks volumes.

✔ **reality check** "Peter Furler (drummer for The Newsboys) speaks of kids turning to Jesus, bringing their lives into line with the ways of God. This is about far more than music, yet it happens because of something that takes place on a stage. You have to wonder: Does Peter Furler ask himself how this scene appears to God? He says, 'One of my biggest fears is to be on my deathbed and then to realize I could have done something different. Christ came to serve. Being in a rock band is not serving. Yet, He uses even this. Which is amazing, and which is why I am so thankful. I'm so unworthy, yet I am under His grace. My life is merely a whisper of the breath of God, but it is His breath, His grace, His life in me.'"

(From *CCM* magazine, August 1997, p. 23)

Word
from the
Word

Let the words of Christ, in all their richness, live in your hearts and make you wise. Use his words to teach and counsel each other. Sing psalms and hymns and spiritual songs to God with thankful hearts. (Colossians 3:16)

DIGGING DEEPER: *Exodus 15:1; Psalms 33:1-3; 66:1-4*

Q: Listening to rock music makes me feel good. What's wrong with that?

A: There is nothing wrong with feeling good. And there's nothing wrong with feeling good while listening to rock music. Some people feel good when they listen to classical music or country music or jazz. Rock is simply a style of music that appeals to some people and not to others. Most adults don't like it because it's too loud and doesn't sound like the music they remember enjoying when they were younger. But that doesn't make it bad music or wrong.

Rock music (and any other kind of music) is wrong when it promotes behavior or values that violate your standards as a Christian. If you are a Christian, then a song that promotes doing drugs, getting drunk, hurting other people, or being sexually immoral shouldn't make you feel very good. On the contrary, a song like that will probably make you feel bad, sad, or angry, or make you want to change radio stations.

So it's all right to feel good, but be careful not to make this the reason for doing everything. Remember, too, that destructive behaviors may feel good in the beginning, but the long-term results of those behaviors don't feel good at all.

Also, consider what *else* the music is doing to you. If you find yourself feeling, thinking, or acting in a wrong way when listening to certain music, don't listen to that kind of music. It's as simple as that.

✔ reality check From the "Did You Know?" files . . .

The theme song for *The NBA on NBC* is called "Roundball Rock" and was written by John Tesh. According to Tesh, the song is written at the same pace as a fast break—one hundred and twenty feet a minute. He says he composed the melody while on a trip to Europe. To keep from forgetting the tune, he called home and sang it to himself on his answering machine. Tesh is considering writing a rap version for an upcoming season. Since he gets royalties every time the song is played, this music must make him feel good!

Word
from the
Word

You furnish lovely music and wine at your grand parties; the harps, lyres, tambourines, and flutes are superb! But you never think about the Lord or notice what he is doing. (Isaiah 5:12)

DIGGING DEEPER: *Proverbs 6:27; Daniel 3:1-18; 1 John 2:15-17*

147

#68

Q: I listen to Christian rock; should I try getting my friends to listen to it?

A: If you enjoy Christian rock music, your friends may very well like it too. Your friends will probably be interested in what interests you, so you should feel free to share your music with them. Don't make it a crusade, however, and push it on them or keep saying that other music isn't good. That may turn them off to anything labeled Christian.

Lots of kids don't know about Christian rock because it doesn't get a lot of exposure on MTV or on the local rock radio stations. That means you'll have to introduce them to the music and the artists. You can do that by taking them to a concert, giving them a CD of your favorite band, or watching some Christian music videos together (if they aren't shown on your local cable TV stations, you can purchase Christian music videos). Most kids are pretty surprised that Christian rock bands are just as good as secular rock bands but without the garbage. There are Christian rock bands that play just about every style of rock there is.

Remember that if you introduce your friends to Christian rock, you just may be introducing them to Christ. What a great way to lead your friends to a relationship with the Lord!

✔ **reality check** You can help your friends find out more about the Christian music scene by reading *CCM* magazine. (*CCM* stands for Contemporary Christian Music.) *CCM* magazine covers a wide range of artists with pop, soul, country, alternative, and traditional sounds. The magazine features interviews with up-and-coming artists, reviews of new releases, concert schedules for most Christian artists, and lots of great articles.

You can probably find a recent copy at your local Christian bookstore, or you can write for subscription info at: *CCM*, P.O. Box 55996, Boulder, CO 80321-0439. *CCM*'s Web site is: http://www.ccmcom.com.

Word
from the
Word

Shout joyful praises to God, all the earth! Sing about the glory of his name! Tell the world how glorious he is. (Psalm 66:1-2)

DIGGING DEEPER: *1 Chronicles 16:8-9; Psalms 67:2-5; 105:1-2*

#69

Q: What's wrong with seeing R-rated movies and videos? I've heard it all and seen it all before.

A: True, you probably have. It's hard to avoid being exposed to all the sex, violence, and evil that are marketed as entertainment these days. But that doesn't mean it's OK to keep on being exposed to it. The Bible says, "Take no part in the worthless deeds of evil and darkness; instead, rebuke and expose them" (Ephesians 5:11). Christians should avoid being entertained or amused by watching people do what is wrong. Most R-rated movies get that rating because even by secular standards there is agreement that the film contains enough sex, violence, or foul language to make it unsuitable for children and teenagers. If the film were rated by Christians, it might get a WOF rating, for "Waste of Film." In other words, you shouldn't bother seeing it, no matter how old you are.

The Bible is also very clear about not filling our minds with garbage. Philippians 4:8 says, "Fix your thoughts on what is true and honorable and right. Think about things that are pure and lovely and admirable. Think about things that are excellent and worthy of praise." We should focus on what is positive and uplifting, not on what is negative, degrading, and sinful. It's like eating—eventually the food you eat affects your physical well-being. If you focus on filling your heart and mind with the right things, you will become a much happier and fulfilled person.

Remember, the fact that you've seen, heard, or done something before doesn't make it OK—you wouldn't apply that rule to being in an automobile accident.

Of course, there are a few movies and videos that, despite the scenes that caused the R rating, are worth seeing. And there are some PG and PG-13 movies that are more harmful than those with an R rating. If a movie is good and you really want to see it, do yourself a favor and wait until an edited version is shown on television.

✔ reality check

"Be smart. Ask around. Check out the posters, the ads. Do they contain scenes that you don't want roaming around inside your mind? Do they touch on a certain weakness you know the Lord is working on? (Violence and profanity have never been problems for me. . . . But since sensuality has always been a battle inside my head, I won't even go near a PG if I know it has sexy situations.)

Again, just be smart. You've only got one mind. Don't let anyone dirty it up."

(From *Hot Topics, Tough Questions* by Bill Myers, p. 83)

Word
from the
Word

You have had enough in the past of the evil things that godless people enjoy—their immorality and lust, their feasting and drunkenness and wild parties, and their terrible worship of idols. (1 Peter 4:3)

DIGGING DEEPER: *2 Kings 17:15; Psalm 101:3-4; Romans 13:13-14*

#70

Q: Does God have a sense of humor?

A: Well, *you* have a sense of humor . . . and you were created in the image of God. Without a doubt, one of God's best gifts to the world is the gift of laughter. Laughter is a uniquely human characteristic, and it comes from God. Ecclesiastes 3:4 says, "A time to cry and a time to laugh. A time to grieve and a time to dance." Obviously, it's better to laugh than to cry, and God wants you to have lots of time for it.

Some people think that God is a grump, always in a bad mood, just waiting to mess up our fun. But that's not true. Jesus said, "My purpose is to give life in all its fullness" (John 10:10). The apostle Paul wrote that Christians should be rejoicing all the time (Philippians 4:4)! God wants you to be full of joy, and one of the ways you experience joy is to enjoy humor. It's a gift from God.

Keep in mind that humor, like other good gifts from God, can be misused. For example, it's wrong to laugh at the misfortunes of others or at jokes that are off-color or that put other people down. Some comedians specialize in humor that is pretty sick. There's nothing wrong with comedy—but when it is immoral or hurtful to others, it's not very funny.

✔ reality check   Nine clues that your youth director may be getting a little old:

1. He thinks he's "styling" in bell-bottoms.
2. She thinks a paintball gun is something you get in a hardware store.
3. He thinks Jars of Clay is a pottery-making group at church.
4. Her idea of contemporary Christian music is anything that includes drums.
5. The first time he saw a kid with a nose ring, he called an ambulance.
6. He thinks MTV means Missionary Travel Vehicle.
7. He uses the flannel graph instead of showing videos.
8. He has more hair in his ears than on his head.
9. The other youth leaders call him mister.

(Adapted from *The Christian Book of Lists* by Randy Petersen, p. 173)

Word *from the* **Word**

And Sarah declared, "God has brought me laughter! All who hear about this will laugh with me." (Genesis 21:6)

DIGGING DEEPER: *Job 8:20-21; Psalm 126:2*

$Q:$ Is God OK with science-fiction books and movies?

$A:$ Science fiction is actually a contradiction in terms (an oxymoron). Science generally is interested only in what can be proven to be true. Fiction, on the other hand, is a story that is not true. So, by definition, science fiction is not "true science."

Science fiction is no different from any other kind of fiction except that it is based on scientific or futuristic themes rather than on historical or romantic themes.

There's nothing wrong with fiction as long as you don't confuse it with reality. Some of the best literature we have is fiction—storytelling. Jesus himself spoke in parables, a form of storytelling. Stories are good, not only for entertainment but also for teaching values and ideas to people. The problem with a lot of science fiction is that it is based on just enough science to make you think it could be true. And much of it teaches or promotes a purely materialistic or atheistic worldview. With the exception of the works of Christian writers, like C. S. Lewis and Madeline L'Engle, it's hard to find God in science fiction.

As with any kind of fiction, the real issue has to do with the values and beliefs being promoted. Just as there are good movies and bad movies, good music and bad music, good books and bad books, there is good science fiction and bad science fiction. Nothing is wrong with science fiction as a category, but if it undermines Christian faith, then it should be avoided.

✔ reality check   The cool thing about science-fiction

literature is that it appeals to the imagination—that bit of your brain that skips over the ho-hum. Because you have been created in God's image, you have a God-given ability to be creative. Get your own creativity in gear! Do you like the out-of-the-ordinary? Could you list your favorite unusual creatures and out-of-this-world settings? Why not try your hand at writing? You could adapt a Bible story using a different setting and cast of characters. Allegory is a kind of story that uses a new situation to retell a meaningful truth. C. S. Lewis's famous book *The Lion, The Witch, and The Wardrobe* does that. So does the entire Chronicles of Narnia series. Maybe someday Christian parents will be encouraging their kids to read your work!

Word *from the* **Word**

Just as the mouth tastes good food, the ear tests the words it hears. (Job 34:3)

DIGGING DEEPER: *Matthew 13:34; Romans 14:14; Philippians 4:8*

Q: If you know that swearing is wrong, is it really bad to hear it in movies?

A: The problem is that the more you hear something that is wrong, the easier it becomes to think that maybe it's not so wrong. Today, bad language is tolerated by more and more people simply because it has become so common. The same is true of sinful behaviors. If you see something in the movies enough times, you will begin to think that maybe it's OK after all. It's natural to become calloused to things that should be very troubling to you.

Sometimes people go to a movie that has a lot of swearing in it and then start using bad language themselves when they come out of the theater. After you've heard a certain word over and over again, you start to think that's the normal way to talk. Like it or not, you are influenced by what you take into your heart and mind through your eyes and ears. Even the strongest Christians can be negatively influenced by the movies and TV shows they watch.

We can't control everything we hear; unfortunately, swearing is part of life—many people swear, and some do so a lot. Because they are trying to portray *real* people, characters in movies often swear. But we should be careful about what we put into our minds, and we can set an example by not swearing ourselves.

Remember that most of the bad language in movies is there simply because the producers of the film think it will attract or shock you. Don't ever think that this is the way decent people talk. You can't really avoid hearing bad language, but whenever you do hear it, use it as a reminder to make a new commitment to yourself to watch what you say. Scripture says that it is wrong for a person to praise God and curse others with the same mouth (James 3:10). Christians who can't control their tongues are only fooling themselves (James 1:26).

✔ **reality check** Here are some other life "realities" that happen only in the movies:

- Landing a plane is easy if there is someone to "talk you down."
- If you need to disguise yourself as a German officer, there's no need to speak the language. A German accent will do the trick.
- If a large pane of glass is in the scene, someone will eventually go through it.
- Should you decide to start dancing in the street, everyone around you will automatically be able to do the steps with you and hear the music playing in your head!

Word
from the
Word

Avoid all perverse talk; stay far from corrupt speech. (Proverbs 4:24)

DIGGING DEEPER: *Ephesians 4:29; 5:4; Colossians 3:8*

157

#73

Q: Can Christians become entertainers in the secular world, or should they only make Christian music and Christian movies?

A: Can a Christian construction worker build secular buildings, or should that person only build churches? Can a Christian athlete play in the NFL, or should he play only for a Christian football league (if one existed)? What about Christian airline pilots, attorneys, or auto mechanics?

God can use Christians in almost every profession. Christians can become lawyers, teachers, doctors, police officers, electricians, and so forth. All of these professions are active in the secular world. It is also good to have Christian entertainers—men and women who work in the secular entertainment business. It's not an easy place to work because of the pressures to live, or represent life, in a non-Christian way, but what better place to be a strong witness for Christ!

Christian artists should do whatever God calls them to do. There are quite a few Christian entertainers who have made an impact on the secular world. In fact, throughout history, some of the world's greatest writers, poets, singers, composers, and actors have been people of faith. This is still true today.

Perhaps if there were more Christians in Hollywood, the movies would be better. Perhaps if there were more Christians in charge of the record companies and more Christian musicians in the secular world, there would be better music on the radio. If Christian artists stop trying to make a difference in the secular world, the world would only get worse, not better.

There is a place for Christian music, movies, books, and theater. If you have musical, writing, or acting talent, you have many more options today than ever before. Remember that God wants you to use your talents and gifts to serve him and bring glory to him. Let him guide you. He may want you to use your gifts to build up and teach Christians, or he may want you to let your light shine in a dark place.

✔ reality check

Austin O'Brien has appeared in movies such as *The Last Action Hero* and *Apollo 13*. He currently plays Joshua Greene on *Promised Land,* a spin-off of the popular series *Touched by an Angel.*

As a Christian, Austin makes careful decisions about the roles he chooses and how the characters are fleshed out on screen. Regarding his current role, he says, "So far, my character has been the only character on *Promised Land* who's actually said, 'I'm a Christian' right on the show. That was important to me. I really believe God has put me in the entertainment business, and he's taken real good care of me along the way. I want to do all I can to give him all the credit."

(From "Living in the Promised Land," *Campus Life* magazine, March/April 1998, p. 41)

Word *from the* **Word**

You are to live clean, innocent lives as children of God in a dark world full of crooked and perverse people. Let your lives shine brightly before them. (Philippians 2:15)

DIGGING DEEPER: *1 Samuel 16:14-23; John 17:15; Titus 2:12*

Getting Through

Q: Since God knows everything, why should I pray?

A: You're right. God does know everything. He knows what you need even before you ask. In fact, he knows what you need even when you don't. According to the Bible, the Holy Spirit prays for us when we don't know what to pray (Romans 8:26).

But that doesn't mean you shouldn't pray. When you pray, you are letting God know that you trust him, that you love him, and that you want to have a close relationship with him. When you pray, you can thank God, ask his forgiveness, pray for others, and just tell him what's on your mind. Prayer is simply conversation with God, a way of staying in touch. Also God has given each person a will, and the fact that he knows what you need doesn't mean that he automatically takes care of it. If you want God's help, he wants you to tell him so.

The most important reason to pray is because God *says* we should pray all the time (see Ephesians 6:18). God desires our prayers, and he wants us to pray regularly (1 Thessalonians 5:17. We don't know *how* prayer works, but we know that it does. Prayer changes us when we pray, and it gets God involved in our lives.

✔ reality check

Prayer is not an argument with God to persuade Him to move things our way, but an exercise by which we are enabled by His Spirit to move ourselves His way.
—*Leonard Ravenhill, pastor and author*

Word
from the
Word

When you pray, don't babble on and on as people of other religions do. They think their prayers are answered only by repeating their words again and again. Don't be like them, because your Father knows exactly what you need even before you ask him! (Matthew 6:7-8)

DIGGING DEEPER: *Psalm 139:4; Ephesians 6:18; 1 Thessalonians 5:17*

#75

Q: **How do I know if God hears what I pray?**

A: The only way we can know for sure that God hears us is to believe the Bible. Many Scriptures assure us that God hears and answers our prayers. Psalm 34:15 says that God is paying close attention to what we have to say. First John 5:14 says, "He will listen to us whenever we ask him for anything in line with his will." If you believe that the Bible is the Word of God, then you can have complete confidence that God hears you when you pray. God tells the truth—we can trust him.

It's helpful to remember that God is able to do what we cannot do. We find it difficult to listen to other people, especially if more than one person is talking, if someone isn't talking loud enough, or if what a person is saying is boring. But God isn't like that. He hangs on your every word—he gives you his undivided attention all the time. That's something your parents, friends, and teachers can't do, and you can't do it for anyone else. But that's what makes God God. He can be everywhere at once, and he can listen closely to what you have to say, even when no one else can.

✔ **reality check**   A friend once asked Mrs. Albert Einstein if she understood the theory of relativity.

"No, not at all," she answered. Then she added with a chuckle, "But I understand Albert, and he can be trusted!" (From *Living and Praying in Jesus' Name* by Dick Eastman and Jack Hayford, p. 9)

Prayer is a greater mystery than the theory of relativity. But don't miss the point. You don't have to write the book on prayer to trust the one who did! Scripture always ties prayer and faith together. The more you grow to know and trust God, the more confidence you will have when you pray.

Word
from the
Word

And we can be confident that he will listen to us whenever we ask him for anything in line with his will. (1 John 5:14)

DIGGING DEEPER: *2 Samuel 22:7; Psalm 91:15; Proverbs 15:29*

Q: Does God hear me if I pray in my head and not out loud?

A: Absolutely! God hears all our prayers—aloud or silent (see Psalms 19:14; 139:23)—so it would be a good idea to pray silently throughout the day. When you are with your friends, in a class at school, or lying in bed at night, you can silently communicate with God by praying "in your head." God is with you and knows what you are thinking. If you direct your thoughts to God, he is pleased with that and will respond to your prayers.

But praying out loud is very useful too. It's good to pray aloud for the benefit of others (in group settings). And it's good to pray out loud for your own benefit. Sometimes it's easier to keep your mind on what you are praying when you pray aloud. If you are just thinking your prayers, it's easy to get distracted and start thinking about other stuff. When you pray out loud, however, it's easier to imagine God sitting there in the room listening to what you have to say. And remember that the Bible encourages us to pray out loud (Romans 10:9-10).

✔ reality check

Here are some thoughts from a young man who has investigated the issue of prayer. This is a portion of a school writing assignment to explain God.

God's second most important job is listening to prayers. An awful lot of this goes on, as some people, like preachers and things, pray other times besides bedtime. God doesn't have time to listen to the radio or TV on account of this. He hears everything, not only prayers. There must be a terrible lot of noise in His ears, unless He has thought of a way to turn it off.

God sees everything and hears everything and is everywhere. This keeps him pretty busy. So you shouldn't go wasting His time by going over your parents' heads and asking for something they said you couldn't have.

You can pray anytime you want and [God] is sure to hear you because [He] is on duty all the time. (Danny Dutton, age 8, Chula Vista, California)

Word
from the
Word

May the words of my mouth and the thoughts of my heart be pleasing to you, O Lord, my rock and my redeemer. (Psalm 19:14)

DIGGING DEEPER: *1 Samuel 1:12-17; Psalm 139:4, 23; Isaiah 65:24*

Q: **How does prayer work? What difference does it make in the world?**

A: How prayer works is something of a mystery. Some people mistakenly believe that prayer is like a magic lamp or a vending machine that will give people whatever they want whenever they want it. But that's not how prayer works because that's not how God works.

The Bible makes it very clear that prayer does make a difference in the world. For example, 2 Chronicles 7:14 says, "Then if my people . . . will humble themselves and pray . . . I will hear from heaven and will forgive their sins and heal their land." Prayer also makes a difference in a person's private world. Jesus said, "Ask, using my name, and you will receive, and you will have abundant joy" (John 16:24). He also said, "You can pray for anything, and if you believe, you will have it" (Mark 11:24).

✔ **reality check** Maybe the question should be: Do we recognize when God answers our prayer?

History books cannot explain why the bombing of London stopped so suddenly in September of 1940. Here is an account from the diary of a London minister known for his praying. You can judge for yourself.

> Day after day the air raid bombing of London continued. From mid-May until September, the citizens of London waited to be invaded while they watched their country being destroyed. Winston Churchill called the country to a Day of Prayer on September 7th. As the meetings began at midday, Nazi planes began passing overhead and the crashing could be heard all around. Though the air raid sirens blasted, the Rev. Howell continued his message. No one in the congregation moved. As the people began to pray, their worries and questions about the past changed into praise. The congregation sensed that victory was certain!
>
> Yet nothing on the outside changed. The bombing continued to escalate. On September 15th, Churchill asked his Air Marshall, "What other reserves do we have?" "There are none, sir," was his response. Victory was within the grasp of the Nazis. Then five minutes passed and reports came that the enemy appeared to be going home. There was no further bombing. In fifteen minutes, the action was over.
>
> Why would the Nazis stop when easy victory was in sight? As Air Chief Marshall Lord Dowding said, "One had the sort of feeling that there had been some sort of Divine intervention."

(From *Rees Howells: Intercessor* by Norman Grubb, pp. 257–262)

Word
from the
Word

The earnest prayer of a righteous person has great power and wonderful results. (James 5:16)

DIGGING DEEPER: *Ezra 8:23; Psalm 107:19; Hebrews 4:16*

#78

Q: Does God always answer our prayers?

A: Absolutely. He may not always answer prayers exactly the way we expected or the way we wanted, but God always hears and answers our prayers. You can trust that God will always do what is right, even though you can't see what he's doing right now. In Matthew 7:9-10 Jesus asks, "You parents—if your children ask for a loaf of bread, do you give them a stone instead? Or if they ask for a fish, do you give them a snake? Of course not!" Likewise, says Jesus, you have a heavenly Father who is even better than you are. He always gives you what is best for you.

When God answers your prayers, you might get a yes and see your prayers answered immediately, just the way you had hoped. Other times you might get a no because God knows something about the situation that you don't know and he is doing what he knows is best. Or, the answer may be wait, which means that you will have to be patient and trust that a clearer answer will come at some later date. Even when God doesn't seem to answer right away, he wants you to keep on praying and believing.

✔ **reality check** Do you think it is a problem for God when members of opposing football teams pray for victory?

Moses once prayed for something that seemed to pose a dilemma. Exodus 33:18-23 tells how Moses made what appeared to be a simple, heartfelt request—to see God. But if God gave Moses what he'd asked for, it would kill Moses. Fortunately, God didn't answer Moses with a yes or no. Was Moses wrong to ask? No. Did God punish him for his request? No, he blessed him. God answered Moses in a way that Moses could handle and that would bring glory to God. God will do the same for you.

So if opposing football teams pray that they will honor God by the way they play, God can answer yes to both teams even though one of them will lose the game.

Word
from the
Word

[Jesus] went on a little farther and fell face down on the ground, praying, "My Father! If it is possible, let this cup of suffering be taken away from me. Yet I want your will, not mine." (Matthew 26:39)

DIGGING DEEPER: *Yes: Psalm 37:4-5; John 15:7.*
No: 2 Corinthians 12:6-9; Deuteronomy 3:23-27.
Wait: Luke 18:7-8; Revelation 6:9-11

Q: What should we pray for/about?

A: Prayer is simply talking with God, just as we would talk to a friend. We can talk to him about anything on our mind. There are two types of prayer: casual and in-depth. In casual prayers, we talk with God throughout the day, whenever we feel like it. In-depth prayers, however, take more time; this is where we really get down to business with God.

When Jesus taught his disciples how to pray, he gave them a model prayer that we call the Lord's Prayer (see Matthew 6:9-13). Actually, it is *our* prayer, because it's an example of how we should pray. The Lord's Prayer helps us know the topics to cover in our in-depth prayers.

First, we address God as "Father." This reminds us that we are his children and that God cares for us and wants to help us grow. Second, we praise God and thank him for his greatness and goodness to us. Third, we let God know that we want to live according to his will and purposes. Fourth, we bring our requests to him. Fifth, we confess our sins. Sixth, we ask for God's protection and guidance. Seventh, and last, we praise God and thank him again for hearing and answering our prayers.

You don't need to follow that outline, but it's helpful to remember that prayer is more than just asking God for stuff. Take time to talk to God, letting him know what's on your heart.

✔ **reality check** History records young people's influence in the world as they prayed for God's power to be shown. One such example is the Jesus movement of the 1970s. High school and college students across America prayed for God to move in extraordinary ways in their personal lives and in their country. The result was that millions of people came to Christ. Young people of that time sensed that their friends and relatives needed better ways to learn about God. Contemporary Christian music was born during the Jesus movement. *The Living Bible* became a valuable tool that made the truth of Scripture understandable. Many Christian ministries came into being as a result of the Jesus movement. And many groups like Campus Crusade for Christ and Young Life experienced great growth during that time.

Would you like to see this happen today? Pray for it!

Word *from the* **Word**

Pray like this: Our Father in heaven, may your name be honored. May your Kingdom come soon. May your will be done here on earth, just as it is in heaven. Give us our food for today, and forgive us our sins, just as we have forgiven those who have sinned against us. And don't let us yield to temptation, but deliver us from the evil one. (Matthew 6:9-13)

DIGGING DEEPER: *Luke 11:1-4.* Father: ***Romans 8:15; Galatians 4:6.*** *Praise: **Psalms 95:2; 100:4.** Yield: **Psalm 143:10; Luke 22:42.** Make Requests: **Philippians 4:19.** Confess Sin: **Job 42:1-5; Psalm 51:1-5; Luke 18:13-14.** Ask for Protection/Guidance: **2 Samuel 22:7; Hebrews 4:16.** Praise/Give Thanks: **Philippians 4:6***

Q: Is there a right way and a wrong way to pray?

ACTUALLY, **THIS** IS THE CORRECT POSITION TO PRAY IN. NOTICE THE KNEE BENT PRECISELY AT A 45-DEGREE ANGLE. BEND IT TWO DEGREES EITHER WAY AND YOU MIGHT AS WELL NOT BOTHER PRAYING.

A: Yes. One "wrong way" to pray is to not pray at all. It really doesn't matter that much to God that you are praying the "right way." He just wants you to pray from your heart. You can pray at any time and in any place or position. With few exceptions, any prayer is good prayer as long as it is sincere and without doubt (James 1:6; 4:3; 1 John 5:14-15). Jesus did warn people about praying just to show off. He criticized hypocrites who stood on the street corners and prayed loudly to impress everybody else with how spiritual they were (Matthew 6:5).

Sometimes it's easy to be intimidated by the fancy prayers you hear at church or from people who are good at praying aloud. Remember, however, that prayer is to be directed to *God*. Don't worry about how it sounds to other people. A prayer is not a speech—it's normal conversation with God. You don't have to pray with special words *(thee's* and *thou's)* or pray for any set length of time. That's why Jesus recommended going into a closet (or any place where you are alone) to pray. God is the only one who needs to hear you pray, and you can just be yourself.

✔ reality check   Consider this:

- Some baseball players never take a bath on game day.
- Michael Jordan still wears his uniform shorts from the University of North Carolina under his Bulls uniform.
- Karl Malone of the Utah Jazz has a secret saying that he repeats before every free throw.
- A former Philadelphia Phillies star added a piece of bubblegum to the existing wad at the start of each inning.

Why do they do it? They're superstitious! In some weird way, they believe it helps their game. In many religions there are super- stitions that people believe will get their prayers answered. For example, holding beads, burning incense, using proper music, bow- ing in a certain direction, repeating phrases, or using a different language are methods that are followed.

The Bible speaks of people bowing, raising hands, lying on the ground, or kneeling. You need to find a comfortable way that helps you concentrate. The good news is that you don't have to find the right combination of factors to make God listen. He *always* listens because he cares for you.

Word
from the
Word

People judge by outward appearance, but the Lord looks at a person's thoughts and intentions. (1 Samuel 16:7)

DIGGING DEEPER: *Matthew 6:6-8.* Neglect: *Isaiah 64:7; James 4:2b.* Doubt: *Matthew 17:19-20; Hebrews 11:6. Insincerity: Matthew 6:5-7.* Pride: *Matthew 6:5; Luke 18:9-14.* Sin: *Psalm 66:18; Micah 3:4*

Q: How come sometimes when I pray it feels like no one is there listening to me?

A: There is an old bumper sticker that says "If you are feeling far away from God, guess who moved?" The point is that if you don't feel close to God or he seems far away, chances are that it has more to do with you than with God. God is always there, and he is always listening, even when we don't feel like he is. God is always the same, but we change. At times you may feel very spiritual and very close to God. When you do, God will seem close to you. But when you are feeling discouraged, full of doubts, short on faith, or just spiritually dry, God will probably seem a long way off. But God hasn't changed or moved at all. He is still there, and he is listening to you. Hint: Keep on praying, and before you know it, you'll recognize God's presence there with you again.

Don't rely on your feelings—trust God.

✔ **reality check** Sometimes we come to God in prayer with some pretty rotten attitudes. It's often easier to see other people's faults than it is to see our own need to change.

Maybe you have something in common with this guy: He walked into a psychiatrist's office sporting a cantaloupe on his head and strips of bacon wrapped around each ear. The psychiatrist thought, *Here's a guy who really needs help.* Then the man with the cantaloupe on his head and the bacon on his ears sat down. "I've come," he said, "to talk to you about my brother. He needs help." (From *The Winning Attitude* by John Maxwell, p. 164)

If our prayers reflect an attitude that we're fine but everyone else needs "improvement," our pride may keep us from feeling God's presence when we pray.

Word
from the
Word

O Lord, why do you stand so far away? Why do you hide when I need you the most? Lord, you know the hopes of the helpless. Surely you will listen to their cries and comfort them. (Psalm 10:1, 17)

DIGGING DEEPER: *Psalms 13:1-3; 27:9; 34:17-18*

#82

Q: **How long should I pray? Is praying once for one thing long enough?**

YESSS SIR!
I'M SURE I'LL GET THAT
RED CORVETTE NOW.
I ASKED GOD FOR IT
743 TIMES!

A: The Bible doesn't say exactly how long your prayers should be, but it does say, "Keep on praying" (1 Thessalonians 5:17). This verse doesn't mean that a person should pray twenty-four hours a day. But it does indicate that prayer is not just a short speech but a continuing conversation with God that goes on all day long. You should pray when you wake up in the morning, when you go to bed at night, and whenever you can during the day. You don't have to pray long prayers. Any length prayer is a good prayer. It's better to pray often than to pray one long prayer and then go on your way without praying again for a long time. To "keep on praying" means that you live with a constant awareness that God is with you and wants to be involved in your life.

Is praying once for one thing long enough? Scripture tells us that we should continue praying for things that we desire from God. Jesus told a story in the Bible about a man who kept pestering his neighbor in the middle of the night for some food until, finally, the neighbor got up and gave the man what he wanted (Luke 11:5-8). Jesus was teaching that we shouldn't stop praying just because our prayers haven't been answered yet. God wants us to keep praying, to not give up on him. That's one of the ways we demonstrate our faith.

A relationship with a close friend cannot grow if communication consists exclusively of casual conversation. Friends also need in-depth talks, time alone together to really get to know each other. It's the same with a relationship with God. We can and should talk with him all the time. To know him well, however, we need to set aside daily time to be alone with him, to really talk things over.

✔ reality check
Does it make sense for you to keep praying for something you already have? You may feel sorry for something you've done or said and you ask God for forgiveness. Because of God's promise in 1 John 1:9, you can know he has answered. You will never have to mention it again. Once is enough.

On the other hand, if you're praying about something that concerns you that has not come to pass, then you should keep asking! Will God be annoyed if you continue to pray for a lost friend? Never! God is moved when our hearts continue to turn to him as our source of help.

Word from the Word

And so I tell you, keep on asking, and you will be given what you ask for. Keep on looking, and you will find. Keep on knocking, and the door will be opened. (Luke 11:9)

DIGGING DEEPER: *1 Kings 18:42-43; Matthew 26:44; Luke 18:1-8*

179

Q: People say, "God spoke to me in prayer." Should I hear God's voice talking to me?

GOD, I'M REALLY LISTENING, BUT I JUST CAN'T HEAR YOU. WHY CAN'T I HEAR FROM YOU?

HOLY BIBLE

A: God does speak to his people in prayer. When God speaks, you probably won't hear his voice out loud. But if you take the time to listen to God, you will recognize his voice. The Bible refers to the "gentle whisper" of God's voice (1 Kings 19:12). This indicates that you must be quiet in order to hear God. Turn off the music, shut out the noise, take some time to be quiet, read from God's Word, and ask God to speak to you; then allow God—through his Holy Spirit—to give you insights and direction for your life. If you are open to it, you will hear God speak to you. He will give you thoughts that are in harmony with his. You won't hear a voice, but you will begin to recognize when God is speaking to you.

Remember that God never contradicts himself. Some people

will say, "God told me" to do this or that, even when those things contradict his Word, the Bible. For example, a person might say that God told him that it's OK to have sex without being married. Obviously, this person wasn't listening to God. God won't tell you to do something or to believe something that contradicts the Bible. But God will often speak to you and help you understand his Word better or apply it to your life. God speaks to us in many ways. He speaks to us through his Word and through other people. He also speaks to us in prayer. If you are truly listening to God, you will recognize his voice.

✔ reality check

Have you ever seen the movie *The Wizard of Oz*? Remember how hard Dorothy, Scarecrow, Tin Man, and Cowardly Lion worked to get an audience with "the great and powerful Oz"? In the end, the Oz was just an ordinary man who had only wisdom and encouragement to offer. But the people weren't interested without the threats, the smoke, the thunder, and the light show.

If you're really interested in hearing God speak to you, he won't have to yell.

Word from the Word

A mighty windstorm hit the mountain. It was such a terrible blast that the rocks were torn loose, but the Lord was not in the wind. After the wind there was an earthquake, but the Lord was not in the earthquake. And after the earthquake there was a fire, but the Lord was not in the fire. And after the fire there was the sound of a gentle whisper. (1 Kings 19:11-12)

DIGGING DEEPER: *God's Voice: 1 Samuel 3:9-10; Luke 2:25-26. The Word: Psalm 119:18; Luke 24:32 Caution: Jeremiah 23:21; Ezekiel 13:6-7*

Q: Why do adults make such a big deal about grades?

"Joni Jackson has A+ average"

A: Parents and teachers want you to do your best, and grades are a teacher's measurement of how well you are doing in class and what you are learning. Adults also care about grades because grades sometimes measure not only how much you know about a particular subject but also what kind of person you are or are going to be. Sometimes students get poor grades because they are lazy and don't study.

All of your life you will have things like grades—standards by which you will be judged. No matter what kind of job or career you eventually have, you will have goals, objectives, requirements, and responsibilities. If you have trouble taking responsibility for getting passing grades now, then you may have trouble taking responsibility for a career or a family or the rest of your life.

Most adults don't really care if you know the capital of Latvia or how to dissect a frog. But they do care that you have shown the ability to show up for class on time, follow instructions, do the work that is assigned, and perform up to your capabilities. You may think that the class is a total waste, but in a very important way it is a small slice of life that will help you grow as a person and be successful.

There is a very good reason why kids who get good grades tend to become the most successful adults in the real world. It's not because they have learned all the subjects really well and can remember everything in those boring textbooks. It's because they have shown that they are responsible, diligent, conscientious, and cooperative people, capable of achieving their goals.

✔ **reality check**   Maybe you'd like to go back to the system that universities followed several hundred years ago. In that system there were no grades, no course of study, no class assignments, no tests. A student was free to meet with the group, listen to the teacher, and work on his own as long as he wished. Graduation was achieved by passing a single oral examination by the school's "master teachers." One chance. It was either thumbs up or back to the drawing board. Very few students were able to stand the pressure or meet the demands. Eventually grades were designed as a kinder system to encourage students to be systematic and disciplined in their classes. If you think your parents make a big deal about grades, think how they'd react to your having to start over after your fifth year in high school!

Word
from the
Word

Work hard and become a leader; be lazy and become a slave. (Proverbs 12:24)

DIGGING DEEPER: *Proverbs 15:19; 20:11; 21:5*

Q: Why do parents get so upset at one bad test if you still have a good grade in the class?

A: Parents are afraid that you may *not* be headed for a good grade. Or they may think you are being lazy and not studying. Good parents want their children to do their best in *everything,* not just have an acceptable grade at the end.

Your goal shouldn't be to just get a "good (enough) grade" but to do your very best. This is an important attitude to cultivate. It reflects something very positive about you: You respect yourself, your classmates, and your teacher enough that you will be the best student you can be.

Remember to work hard on every assignment and test. You may think that since you are doing OK in a class, you can forget one test and get away with it. But what if you have trouble with another test? or another? Suddenly the good grade isn't so good anymore.

The problem with not doing well on one test is that the material you didn't learn will probably show up again on a final, or you will need to know that material to do well on the next test. Sometimes a test can be like a link in a chain. Without that one little link, the chain is broken and becomes useless.

Your parents probably worry because they don't know if your "one bad test" will be the only one or not. Several bad tests (and ultimately a bad grade) always start out as "one bad test." It's better to be concerned at the beginning than to be sorry when it's too late to do anything about it.

✔ reality check   Right now I'm having amnesia and deja vu at the same time. I think I've forgotten this before!

> I think sleeping was my problem in school. If school had started at 4:00 in the afternoon, I'd be a college graduate today.
> —*George Foreman, former boxer*

Word *from the* **Word**

God gave these four young men an unusual aptitude for learning the literature and science of the time. (Daniel 1:17)

DIGGING DEEPER: *Proverbs 4:1-2; 10:5; 28:19*

Q: Will God be mad if I drop out of school?

A: God wants you to do your best and to use and invest well the gifts he has entrusted to you. Dropping out of school will hurt you and your chances for success.

The Bible doesn't have a commandment that says you have to graduate from high school or college. That's because no high schools or colleges existed in Bible times. Jesus probably was taught at home by his parents, or he went to the synagogue and the temple to learn what he needed to know (Luke 2). In either case, he received his education in an organized manner, just like you do in your school.

But there's no question that God wants us to learn all we can so we can live up to the potential that he has given us. These days, a person really needs to have an education in order to get anywhere at all in life. Without a high school or college diploma, it's hard to get a good job and be successful in a career. While the Bible never mentions high school or college, it does tell us to study hard in order to get God's approval and avoid being ashamed in front of others (2 Timothy 2:15).

God may not be mad at you for dropping out of school, but you may be mad at yourself one day. Certainly if you have the ability and the opportunity to get a good education, you should do so. There are many young people around the world who don't have the opportunity to go to school and would give anything to be able to.

If school is difficult for you, just think of the strength of character that you will gain from not giving up, from finishing what you started, and from doing your best.

✔ **reality check** Dave Thomas, founder of Wendy's Restaurants, was a high school dropout. In his book, *Well Done! The Common Guy's Guide to Everyday Success,* he says this about his experience: "Because I was a dropout, I learned what it meant to work hard very early in life. Dropouts are unacceptable in society; people look down on them. It didn't take me long to learn that dropouts had to work harder just to get by and superhard to break through."

Word *from the* **Word**

And you will say, "How I hated discipline! If only I had not demanded my own way! Oh, why didn't I listen to my teachers? Why didn't I pay attention to those who gave me instruction?" (Proverbs 5:12-13)

DIGGING DEEPER: *Proverbs 4:25-26; 19:20; 23:12*

Q: **Does God really help me when I pray before a test?**

A: If you have paid attention in class, taken good notes, and studied hard, then, yes, God will help you. Prayer won't guarantee an A on the test, but God will be with you, and he will help you to remember what you have learned. But no amount of prayer will help you to miraculously remember stuff you haven't learned. God won't rescue you from the consequences of poor study habits. Also, God wants to help us learn, grow, and be our best. If he did everything for us, we wouldn't learn or grow very much.

So before taking a test, pray and ask God to help you concentrate, remember, relax, and do your best. The best time to begin praying about doing well on a test is when you first start learning the information.

✔ **reality check** Getting ready for a test is like climbing steps in a three-story building. You couldn't jump from the ground floor to the third floor, could you? Get yourself in shape for the last flight of stairs by making a steady climb:

Warm-up. (1) Pay attention in class! You snooze, you lose. (2) Take notes in your own words. (3) Find a quick way to review your notes each day. Try reading them into a tape recorder.

Get your brain pumping. (1) Complete your homework at home. (2) Do the hardest subject first. (3) Take a break between subjects. (4) Write down key words, phrases, and definitions from reading assignments and summarize each section before you move on. (5) Stick with it until the assignment is *completely* finished.

Go for the top flight. Find interesting ways to review for the test. (1) Put an important phrase or concept to music. (2) Make a nonsense sentence to recall a list of names (Planets in the Solar System: My Very Energetic Mother Just Served Us New Pickles). (3) Create flash cards for yourself. Study the cards that don't "light up" your memory. (4) Cue yourself to review. Attach a difficult part of the material to something you do several times a day (tie your shoes, brush your teeth, open the refrigerator) and go over the information each time you do it. (5) Study with a partner who stays on track. (6) Don't cram the night before. Get a good night's rest.

Now, ask God to help with your test. He has promised to reward those who sincerely seek him (Hebrews 11:6).

(Adapted from "Study Smart: An Aerobic Workout" by Maria T. Abissi, *Brio* magazine, September 1997)

Word *from the* **Word**

Take a lesson from the ants, you lazybones. Learn from their ways and be wise! Even though they have no prince, governor, or ruler to make them work, they labor hard all summer, gathering food for the winter. (Proverbs 6:6-8)

DIGGING DEEPER: *Proverbs 12:11; 14:23; 21:5*

Q: Is it illegal to take a Bible to class?

A: No, there is no law that prohibits taking a Bible to school or to class. The only reasons a teacher or anyone else might have a problem with your taking a Bible to class would be if you were reading it when you should be reading your class text, doing an assignment, or paying attention to the teacher, or if you were preaching to classmates during class time. But there's no reason why you can't take a Bible to school or carry it to class. In fact, it would be a good way to let other students know that you are a Christian and that the Bible is important to you. Taking a Bible to class might lead to some discussions with other students during lunch or after school about your faith in Christ. When you get that opportunity, share your faith with love (1 Peter 3:15).

✔ **reality check** The American Center for Law and Justice is a public-interest law firm and educational organization that works to protect the rights of Christian believers in the culture. The following is a list of ten freedoms guaranteed to students under the first amendment:

1. Freedom to meet with other students for prayer, Bible study, and worship
2. Freedom to wear religious T-shirts, symbols, and buttons at school
3. Freedom to share your religion on campus
4. Freedom to hand out religious tracts on campus
5. Freedom to engage in voluntary school prayer
6. Freedom to bring your Bible to school
7. Freedom to present school projects from a religious perspective
8. Freedom to study and practice religious holidays on campus
9. Freedom to have religious clubs on campus
10. Freedom to live out your religious faith

(From www.aclj.org, © 1997 by Jay Sekulow and the American Center for Law and Justice. ARR.)

Word *from the* **Word**

For I am not ashamed of this Good News about Christ. It is the power of God at work, saving everyone who believes—Jews first and also Gentiles. (Romans 1:16)

DIGGING DEEPER: *2 Chronicles 17:9; Acts 17:2, 18-20*

Q: Should I disagree with my teacher when he teaches evolution?

A: As a Christian, you believe the Bible to be the Word of God, and that includes believing that God created the world. The Bible doesn't go into great detail about how God created everything, but it *is* clear that God was the creator.

Learning about evolution doesn't mean that you have to stop believing in God the Creator, but you may need to take a stand. Explain your position, and let your teacher know what you believe. You'll probably be able to believe the biblical version of creation and still pass the course. Actually, you shouldn't be afraid to at least hear about evolution and learn what it's about. It's not smart for Christians to pretend that the theory doesn't exist. Learn what evolution is about—that probably will help you answer questions about what you believe. But don't believe anything that denies the existence and creative activity of God.

If your teacher allows for questions and discussion during class time take the opportunity to share what you believe. In some schools, teachers are forced to teach evolution, but they aren't allowed to teach the biblical view of creation. However, students can bring it up. Be prepared ahead of time to answer any questions your teacher might ask you. (People put a lot of effort into learning the theory of evolution, so we Christians should apply ourselves in learning what the Bible teaches.) If it appears that your teacher or classmates want to argue or put you down, be gracious and avoid getting into a fight.

✔ **reality check** Look, your teachers and friends won't go for the "cause my dad said so" defense. There is a lot of good material available on the creation-vs.-evolution debate, and you won't need a Ph.D. to understand it.

The Institute for Creation Research was founded in 1970 to meet the need for research, publication, and teaching in fields of science related to the issues of the biblical view of creation. Check out their Web site at: www.icr.org for a list of resources, information on seminars, a schedule of the institute's radio show, and lots of other cool stuff!

The book *Defeating Darwinism by Opening Minds* by Philip E. Johnson was written to guide junior and senior high students through science-class discussions. The author shows that not all reasoning by evolutionists is sound, and he helps students overcome the intimidation factor that keeps Christians from speaking out.

Word
from the
Word

The Lord, your Redeemer and Creator, says: "I am the Lord, who made all things. I alone stretched out the heavens. By myself I made the earth and everything in it." (Isaiah 44:24)

DIGGING DEEPER: *Isaiah 48:12-13; Hebrews 11:3; 1 Peter 3:15*

Q: How important is it to make your Christianity known in your school?

A: It's very important. Let people see the difference in your life, and then "be ready to explain" what you believe (1 Peter 3:15).

Most public schools don't allow teachers or students to promote religion on campus. Schools try to stay neutral so they don't offend anyone or discriminate against those who have different views. But that doesn't mean you can't share Christ with your friends personally, wear a Christian pin or symbol, carry a Bible to school, or invite someone to a Bible study or youth group. There are many ways that you can make Christianity known to others without breaking the rules or doing something that might reflect badly on the gospel. You can do this by being kind and cooperative, by helping those whom no one else wants to help, by refusing to gossip, and so forth.

Keep in mind that as a Christian you are making Christianity known all the time, not just at school. You do that, not just by talking about it or distributing Christian literature, but by your deeds, how you live. That's what it means to be a witness for Christ. You shouldn't change the way you live at school just because school is off-limits for religious activities. Keep on living for Christ in front of your friends and teachers, and you will be making Christianity known in the best way possible.

You might also use your church youth group, Campus Life, Young Life, Fellowship of Christian Athletes, See You at the Pole, and other Christian organizations and events to reach out to your classmates.

✔ reality check   What is "See You at the Pole"?

SYATP began early in 1990 when some groups of high school youths near Ft. Worth, Texas, began meeting at their school to pray. Later that year, twenty thousand teenagers at Reunion Arena in Dallas were challenged to meet at their flagpole on a September morning. When more than forty-five thousand students on twelve hundred campuses turned out to pray, SYATP was born!

By 1998 3 million or more students on at least five continents gathered to lift up local, national, and global concerns. At some schools the before-school prayer continues on a daily basis. Bible studies have been formed, and more than ten thousand student-led Christian clubs have been started.

Isn't it cool to find out that someone else is a follower of Christ too? Don't miss this chance to let yourself be known to others!

Word
from the
Word

Instead, you must worship Christ as Lord of your life. And if you are asked about your Christian hope, always be ready to explain it. But you must do this in a gentle and respectful way.
(1 Peter 3:15-16)

DIGGING DEEPER: *Psalm 119:42; Philippians 2:14-15; Titus 2:7-10*

#91

Q: Why do I have to take all these stupid classes that I'll never use in the future?

> LET'S SEE: AT 380 DEGREES, IT TAKES A BURGER
> 5 MINUTES TO COOK, TAKING INTO
> CONSIDERATION THAT EACH BURGER IS ONLY
> 4.21% FAT. COOKING SURFACE IS ... EACH BURGER
> IS ... IN DIAMETER ... LET'S SEE (x-216..794)=
> Pi = 21.86 HMMM ...

A: Actually, you *may* use the classes in the future—you never know. Even if you think you know for sure what your future career will be, remember that sometimes adults change careers, some several times. But "using" a class in the future is not the only reason to take it—classes help you grow and mature, teach you how to think, and give you options.

Most schools require you to take a variety of courses so you will be become a well-rounded, well-educated person. Even though you may think you don't need history right now, some-day you will appreciate knowing something about the govern-ment or Alexander the Great. You may wonder why anyone would want to know how to determine the area of a rectangle, but when you learn to do that, you will also be learning how to measure a room for buying wallpaper or carpet.

School is a lot more than learning what's in your textbooks. It's also about discipline, hard work, achieving goals, developing relationships with other people, and learning how to think. By being exposed to a wide variety of subjects and experiences and ideas, you will have the opportunity to discover exactly what you want to do with your life. The classes you take now may seem stupid, but wait a few years. You'll be glad you took them.

✔ **reality check** Hey, lighten up! Here are some inventions by people who wasted their time on stupid stuff. . . .

- The Chewing Brush—Created for people whose hands are just too busy to hold a toothbrush. Comes with a gentle reminder to "spit, don't swallow!"
- The Backward/Forward Shoe—The top of the shoe looks normal, but the sole faces backward (heel under toe). Why? To throw anyone who is following you off track.
- The Thumb Twiddler—When you put your thumbs into either end of the cylinder, this marvelous tool will count your thumb rotations. Can you hear your mom saying, "I'm very disappointed in the drop in your twiddling totals. You have to do better"?

(From *Actual Factuals for Kids* by Nancy Hill, pp. 124–125)

Word *from the* **Word**

Be sure to stay busy and plant a variety of crops, for you never know which will grow—perhaps they all will. (Ecclesiastes 11:6)

DIGGING DEEPER: *Proverbs 5:12-13; 15:2*

Q: My parents want me to go to college and only care about academics. I'm interested in sports and art. I really want to go to art school, not college. Do I listen to my parents or do what I know is best for me?

A: If you are gifted in athletics or in art and if you are certain that you want to pursue a career as a professional athlete or artist, then you first need to prove yourself to your parents by excelling in those areas. Work hard at perfecting your athletic or artistic skills so that your parents (and others, too) will recognize your talent and encourage you in those areas. Just being interested in sports or art is not enough. You need to demonstrate that you have the talent and the desire it takes to succeed.

Your parents are probably concerned that you have a good, well-rounded education so you can make a good living at whatever you choose to do. Even athletes and artists can benefit greatly from a good education. Most colleges that produce great athletes also require that they do well in academics. In fact, the most successful athletes are those who have applied themselves in the classroom as well as on the athletic field. The same is true for artists. The greatest artists are people who are knowledgeable in many areas, not just art.

Your parents know you pretty well; remember, they've known you all your life. So talk to them about your dreams and desires. If you are serious about what you want to do with your life and the kind of education you feel you need, try your best to communicate that to them and then back it up with your actions. If your parents disagree with you now, be patient. When you are older, you'll have the freedom to make more choices on your own, and you'll probably be able to pursue the career that you feel is best for you. It's never too late.

✔ reality check

Have you examined your scorecard on knowing what is best for you? Most people wouldn't want those stats printed in the sports section!

Your parents want you to keep as many options open for yourself as possible. Ask some college juniors or seniors if they changed their major after they started college. Did you know that lots of people change direction more than once during those years? After you've spent a year in college, continue to keep the lines of communication open with your parents. Perhaps they will feel more confident of your direction and agree to a different strategy.

Word
from the
Word

Plans succeed through good counsel; don't go to war without the advice of others. (Proverbs 20:18)

DIGGING DEEPER: *Proverbs 13:12-13; Daniel 6:3*

#93

Q: If God is love, why is there so much hate?

A: You are right. God is love (1 John 4:8). He is the author and creator of love, and he himself loves perfectly. That's why many people over the centuries have asked the questions, "How did hate get here? Didn't God create everything?"

God created human beings with the freedom to choose between good and evil. God could have created everyone like robots or windup dolls. Instead, God in his goodness created us with the ability to choose between right and wrong. Unfortunately, from the very beginning (Adam and Eve) we have chosen the wrong. In fact, since that first sin, every human being is born into the world as a sinner, with a sin nature. And sinners do what comes naturally to them— they sin. When people choose to live apart from God, the world becomes filled with sin and hate.

If God had wanted to eliminate the possibility of sin, he could have made us inanimate, like he did the rocks and the trees, or he could have just not created us at all. And if God had wanted to eliminate sin after the fact, he could have eliminated humankind. God could simply have wiped us all out. But God chose another way. He provided a way for us to be saved from our sin: God sent his Son, Jesus, to die on the cross. God now invites us to be changed by trusting in Christ as our Savior.

The only way to get rid of hate in the world is to let the love of God take away our sin and to gradually be changed into people who are able to love more consistently. That's something you can choose to do.

✔ **reality check** What examples come to your mind when you think of the word *hate?* Racism? Hitler? Gang violence? The KKK? Skinheads? War?

Our introduction to the word *hate* in Scripture has nothing to do with broad groups of people or evil madmen. Instead, the first hate occurs within families, among brothers. The stories of Cain and Abel (Genesis 4:1-12), Esau and Jacob (Genesis 25:27-34), and Joseph and his brothers (Genesis 37:2-4) give a picture of hate and betrayal stemming from something as common as jealousy. Why is there so much hate? We have to look very closely at ourselves. Hate starts in the hearts of very normal people.

Word *from the* **Word**

Let us continue to love one another, for love comes from God. Anyone who loves is born of God and knows God. But anyone who does not love does not know God—for God is love. (1 John 4:7-8)

DIGGING DEEPER: *Galatians 5:16-26; Ephesians 2:2-4; James 4:1-4*

Q: Why does God allow so much pain and suffering?

I REALLY DON'T THINK GOD HAD ANYTHING TO DO WITH THAT!

A: There are no easy answers to this question. Part of the problem is that we can't see things from God's perspective. One thing we do know: God is all-powerful. If he wanted to, he could take all the pain and suffering in the world and do away with it. But he doesn't. So it must have a purpose, and God surely knows what it is.

God could have created a world without pain and suffering, but he gave us the ability to choose between good and evil. The Bible says, "All have sinned; all fall short of God's glorious standard" (Romans 3:23). Pain and suffering are the result of sin in the world. And sometimes even innocent people suffer because of that sin. Unborn children who are aborted, for example, have not committed sins of their own, but they suffer because of a sinful world.

God has promised to eliminate pain and suffering someday. If we believe in Jesus Christ and accept God's free gift of salvation, we will one day go to heaven where "there will be no more death or sorrow or crying or pain" (Revelation 21:4).

✔ **reality check** God doesn't expect us to run for first place in the suffering line. That wouldn't really make sense. But many people who have experienced great suffering have seen God's power displayed in life-changing ways.

A strange disease was spreading through the tribe where a missionary doctor served. It became clear that the entire tribe would be wiped out. With only the most basic medical tools, the missionary doctor could only ease the suffering and comfort the families. He prayed for guidance, he begged for God to intervene, and he watched people die. The doctor petitioned the U.S. government for help. He wanted some of the patients to be brought to the U.S. for study. But U.S. law would not permit it.

Before long the missionary doctor began to exhibit symptoms of the deadly disease. The mission board immediately flew the broken-hearted doctor to the States. Now his role became the research "guinea pig" into the mysterious disease. Within a short time, scientists had found the cause and developed an antidote. The missionary doctor recovered and took the medicine back to his mission post and saved the tribe.

By the way, the illness left the doctor without vision in one eye. He says it reminds him that we can never see the full picture in the middle of suffering.

Word from the Word

I have told you all this so that you may have peace in me. Here on earth you will have many trials and sorrows. But take heart, because I have overcome the world. (John 16:33)

DIGGING DEEPER: *Fallen World: **Genesis 3:16-19.** Result of Sin: **Job 4:8; James 4:1-2.** Victory: **Romans 8:18, 38-39; Revelation 21:4***

Q: Since God can do anything, why doesn't he make things fair? I don't want special treatment; I just want things fair.

A: God is fair and perfectly just, but the world isn't fair. Life never has been fair since Adam and Eve decided to commit the first sin in the Garden of Eden. Since then, people have been "looking out for number one." In other words, people are basically selfish. That's because they're sinners. No one is born with the tendency to be fair. Instead, we are selfish; we all want what's best for *us*. A world filled with selfish people will be very unfair as people look out for themselves first.

If God were *really* going to make things "fair," all of us would get what we deserve: God's judgment because of our sin. Instead, God loved us in spite of our selfishness and sin and sent his Son to save us. That's why Jesus came. It wasn't fair for him to have to die on the cross for our sins because he was the only one who *never* sinned, but he did it so that we could have eternal life. When we believe in him and ask him to live through us, we are given the power to show fairness to others first and to demonstrate the love of God in the world. But we can't do it on our own. We can do it only with God's help.

✔ **reality check** Be sure that you know what you're asking. "Fairness" feels much better when it's in our favor than when it's in the other person's favor. We ask for fairness because we see our own point of view. Often what seems fair to us may look like "special treatment" to others. Who decides what's fair? Think about what it would be like if everything were really "fair."

- No one would go to heaven.
- No one would ever be forgiven.
- There would never be a "first place" again.
- It would be good-bye to grading on the curve.
- It would be hello to a lot more chores.

Jesus has promised us something much better than fairness. He's given us mercy.

Word *from the* **Word**

He has not punished us for all our sins, nor does he deal with us as we deserve. For his unfailing love toward those who fear him is as great as the height of the heavens above the earth. (Psalm 103:10-11)

DIGGING DEEPER: *Psalms 78:37-39; 130:3-4.* Selfishness: *James 4:1-2*

Q: Why isn't the world any different since Jesus came and died? I thought that was supposed to change things.

A: Actually, everything *has* changed because of Christ. Can you imagine what the world would be like if he had not come? Christianity has powerfully influenced government, business, the arts, education, medicine, science, and the list goes on. The greatest universities and hospitals in the world were founded by the church. As missionaries have taken the gospel around the world, they have brought Christian charity to millions of the poor and oppressed. The work and influence of Christians have helped to cure many deadly diseases, abolish slavery, and topple evil dictatorships. It's hard to imagine, but before Christ, the world was a pretty barbaric place. Things could have gotten worse, not better. But Jesus came. When Jesus was born in Bethlehem, died on Calvary, and rose from the dead, the entire world felt the impact, and it is still feeling it today.

Most important, if Christ had not come, you would have no hope at all. There would be no way for you to receive forgiveness for your sins, to find peace with God, to experience his love and grace, to know the joy of serving him, to have eternal life. Yes, there have been lots of changes in the world since Jesus came, but the biggest change of all takes place in the lives of individual people when they place their faith and trust in him. Then those changed people are able to change the world.

✔ reality check

A story is told about a distinguished evangelist who was confronted by a young atheist on the street one day. "Sir," said the young man, "how can you honestly promote this foolishness? Can't you see that all you're promoting is a fake promise that life will get better? I am challenging you to a public debate on the evidence for your faith!"

The older gentleman replied, "I'll gladly accept your challenge, young man. Is this evening at 8:00 acceptable to you?"

"Excellent!" replied the challenger. "I wouldn't miss it."

As the young man walked away, the evangelist called after him, "One more thing, young man. This evening I'll be bringing one hundred men and women along to give examples of how their lives have changed since they trusted Christ. Will you be willing to do the same? If a hundred is too many, one person will do."

That evening the debate hall was filled with people eager to tell how Christ had changed their lives. Unfortunately, the debate never took place. Neither the atheist nor his witness ever arrived.

Word
from the
Word

[Jesus] came once for all time, at the end of the age, to remove the power of sin forever by his sacrificial death for us. (Hebrews 9:26)

DIGGING DEEPER: *Hope in Christ:* **Romans 5:2; Colossians 1:5; Titus 2:12-13.** *Christian Influence:* **Deuteronomy 18:18-20; Proverbs 11:10-11**

#97

Q: **Why did my parents' generation leave the world in such a mess?**

A: Because their parents didn't make them clean their rooms when they were kids. Just kidding!

Every generation has had its own mess to clean up. When your parents were your age, they probably didn't appreciate inheriting the war in Vietnam, the struggle at home for civil rights, the threat of nuclear war, the cold war with the Soviet Union, and the poverty and pollution that continue to be a problem today.

On the positive side, every generation gets the opportunity to leave the world a little better off than before. Even though there are still lots of problems that need to be solved, there are lots of good people doing good things to make the world a better place.

The world has always been messed up, mainly because Satan

continues to work hard, messing up everything he can. Christians are in the world to be "salt and light" (Matthew 5:13-14). Salt acts as a preservative, keeping things from getting worse. We do that by being involved in good works. Light exposes Satan for who he is and points people to Christ. Our challenge is to avoid becoming messed up by the world ourselves and to be a part of God's plan to establish his kingdom here on earth. We pray, "May your Kingdom come soon. May your will be done here on earth, just as it is in heaven" (Matthew 6:10). When we are serving God and doing good works, we are part of God's answer to that prayer.

✔ reality check
How often do you hear people criticizing how *they* have fouled up something? It is easier to say that a whole *generation* has failed. Since the problem is so big, no one can do better this time around either. So why bother? A famous atheist once said that everything he would ever be in life was determined by the time he was sixteen. After that, nothing would change.

That's not what the Bible tells us. God promises that he has hopeful plans for our future (Jeremiah 29:11). When we trust Christ, no matter what age we are, new will replace old in our lives. Everyone—one person at a time—gets the chance to make a difference. So don't waste your time looking at the failures of others. Start making a positive difference today!

Word
from the
Word

Don't long for "the good old days," for you don't know whether they were any better than today. (Ecclesiastes 7:10)

DIGGING DEEPER: Job 8:8-10. *All Sinners:* **Romans 3:23; 1 John 1:8**

Q: What can one person my age do to make a difference in the world?

A: Sometimes it can be pretty discouraging when we look at the world with all its problems. We may wonder how we could possibly do anything to make a difference. That's exactly what Satan wants us to think. But if you are willing to be used by God, you can't help but make a difference in the world.

There is a story in the Bible about a boy who gave Jesus his lunch, and Jesus turned around and fed five thousand people with it (Mark 6:41-44). In the same way, God can take whatever you do and use it in a powerful way to make a difference in the world.

Remember that you have to start with yourself. Make up your mind to do what God wants you to do, no matter how small it may seem or how young you are. God will then give you opportunities to do great things for him.

✔ reality check   Check out these things you can do
to make a *big* difference in the world:

- Sponsor a needy child (Compassion, World Vision, etc.).
- Write letters to prisoners.
- Visit an elderly person from time to time to talk and run errands.
- Plant trees or pick up trash.
- Pray for a friend.
- Teach a Sunday school class.
- Help out at a soup kitchen.
- Raise money to send a missionary a "Christmas bonus."
- Visit someone who is sick.
- Give friends a ride home after a party.
- Sit with a lonely kid at lunchtime.
- Help others with their chores.
- Help out in the church nursery.
- Give a friend a tape of a Christian rock group.
- Write a letter to an elected official.
- Pray for your youth pastor.
- Go on a mission trip.

Just begin where you are. Do what you can—pray—live for Christ. The world is changed one person at a time.

Word
from the
Word

During the eighth year of his reign, while he was still young [sixteen], Josiah began to seek the God of his ancestor David. Then in the twelfth year, he began to purify Judah and Jerusalem, destroying all the pagan shrines. (2 Chronicles 34:3)

DIGGING DEEPER: *1 Samuel 2:18; John 6:3-13; 1 Timothy 4:11-12*

#99

Q: Will we be held responsible for things we didn't do as well as for things we did do?

A: Because the Ten Commandments are mostly "Thou shalt nots," many people think that sins are when you do what you aren't supposed to do. But in the New Testament Jesus gave two new commandments that are not "thou shalt nots" but "thou shalts." He said the two greatest commandments are these: First, love God with all your heart, mind, and soul; second, love your neighbor as yourself (Luke 10:27). This seems to indicate that true religion has a lot more to do with what we *do* than with what we don't do.

Jesus taught these commandments in many of his parables. For example, in Matthew 25 he tells about a man who gave each of his servants some money (talents) to invest and use wisely. Two of the servants did and were rewarded by the man. But one servant hid his talent in the ground and did nothing with it. He was severely punished. Here's the point: God wants you to use the talents and resources he has given you to advance his kingdom.

In Matthew 25:42-43 Jesus says, "I was hungry, and you didn't feed me. I was thirsty, and you didn't give me anything to drink. I was a stranger, and you didn't invite me into your home. I was naked, and you gave me no clothing. I was sick and in prison, and you didn't visit me." When Jesus was asked when all this had happened, he said, "I assure you, when you refused to help the least of these my brothers and sisters, you were refusing to help me" (Matthew 25:45).

So, yes, you will be held responsible for not doing things that are right, just as you will be held responsible for doing things that are wrong. But remember this. You can't possibly do all that is required of you. Nobody is able to live the Christian life perfectly. That's why Jesus died on the cross. Jesus knew that you couldn't live up to God's high standards, so he paid your penalty in advance for all the sins you'll ever commit and the good works that you'll never do.

Does that mean you don't have to do any good deeds? No, not at all. Your good deeds are the evidence (proof) that you have accepted God's free gift of salvation. You are saved by faith, not by good deeds, but faith without good deeds is useless (James 2:20).

✔ reality check
Encouraged by a stirring sermon on right living, some church members began to confess and repent before the congregation. One man stood and said, "I've been smoking three packs of cigarettes a day, and I'm going to quit." Another man promised, "I've been drinking beer, and I'm going to quit." A third church member added, "I've been swearing an awful lot. I'm going to quit!" In the emotion of the moment, a little old lady stood and promised the group, "I haven't been doing *anything,* and I'm going to quit!"

Maybe she's closer to being on track than she thinks!

Word
from the
Word

Remember, it is sin to know what you ought to do and then not do it. (James 4:17)

DIGGING DEEPER: *Matthew 25:31-46; James 2:20*

217

#100

Q: Should Christians ever "pull the plug"?

A: Christians hold a very high view of human life. God created human beings in his image and likeness (Genesis 1:27), and he has commanded us not to commit murder (Exodus 20:13). That's why Christians oppose such practices as abortion (terminating the life of an innocent unborn child) or euthanasia (ending the life of someone who may be terminally ill or suffering greatly.) Euthanasia is sometimes called mercy killing.

While the Bible doesn't specifically mention these practices, there is no indication that God would approve of them. People in desperate situations in the Bible sometimes wished to die. Jonah told the Lord, "I'd rather be dead than alive" (Jonah 4:3) because things were not going the way he had planned. But God had other plans for Jonah. Often he has other plans for us. There is always hope, even when things seem to be irreversible.

Some Christians, however, have left instructions (in the form of a "living will"), telling their children or doctors not to use "extraordinary means" to keep them alive should they ever become injured so badly that the damage is irreversible. In most cases, this means that the brain is dead but the heart may still be beating. This is passive euthanasia, which is, in essence, "pulling the plug." The important thing to remember is that a decision such as this is always difficult and should never be taken lightly.

✔ reality check

Jack Kevorkian and his lawyers had sneered at Project Life, but the people of Detroit would soon be given a lesson in what true Christian compassion looks like. "Before you pick up that telephone to schedule . . . a consultation with Jack Kevorkian, call Project Life." Project Life began in the heart of the Archbishop of Detroit, Cardinal Maida, as a way to provide alternatives for people considering suicide or abortion. The cardinal promised the funds of the church and the support of thirty local agencies to anyone who called for help.

Euthanasia groups claim that when people are suffering, helping them kill themselves is the only "compassionate" response. *Real* compassion is caring for them for months or even years—and, as Mother Teresa put it so well, "letting [them] see Jesus in the midst of [their] suffering."

(From *Burden of Truth* by Charles Colson, pp. 4–5)

Word *from the* **Word**

Do not murder. (Exodus 20:13)

DIGGING DEEPER: *Psalms 31:14-15; 48:14; 90:1-12*

Q: **What about capital punishment?**

A: There is quite a lot of disagreement among Christians regarding this issue. Those who argue against capital punishment usually make these points: (1) It is unfair because only those who can't afford a good attorney are ever executed. (2) It violates the sanctity of human life. (3) Criminals should be cured, not killed. (4) Execution is a "cruel and unusual punishment." (5) It violates the law of love and mercy that Jesus taught in the New Testament.

Those who argue in favor of capital punishment usually believe: (1) It is biblical. "Yes, you must execute anyone who murders another person, for to kill a person is to kill a living being made in God's image" (Genesis 9:6). (2) It serves as a deterrent to serious crime. (3) It protects innocent people from repeat offenders. (4) Jesus never abolished the law and never specifically abolished capital punishment. (5) It affirms the sanctity of life because it punishes those who would take it.

Capital punishment is one of those confusing issues that you will have to decide for yourself. All of the arguments above are persuasive, and there are many others for both sides. There are no simple solutions. But as you develop your personal beliefs and attitudes about life, you will gain a clearer understanding of moral issues like this one. Don't let other people tell you how or what to think about capital punishment or any other issue. Study the Scriptures yourself, stay close to God, and read and listen to what the people you respect have to say. Then decide for yourself what you believe is right.

✔ **reality check**   No matter which side of the argument you support, Jesus has given clear direction about how prisoners should be treated. In Matthew 25:35-40, Jesus said that caring for people in jail is the same as caring for him in person. Can you imagine how your life would be different if your father or mother were in jail? Think about how your holidays and birthdays would change. How would your family survive financially?

Prison Fellowship Ministries is an organization that tries to serve both the prisoner and the prisoner's family. One program in Prison Fellowship's ministry is called Project Angel Tree. Project Angel Tree collects gifts for children of prisoners so the parents can give them a gift at Christmas. Ask your family if you can participate this year. You can request information about other Prison Fellowship Ministries to prisoners by writing to Prison Fellowship Ministries, P.O. Box 17500, Washington, D.C. 2004-0500 or at their Web site: www.pfm.org.

Word *from the* **Word**

Each person should have a personal conviction about this matter. (Romans 14:5)

DIGGING DEEPER: *Pro: **Leviticus 24:17, 21; Numbers 35:16-31.** Con: **Matthew 5:43-47; John 1:17; Hebrews 8:13***